Spatial
Reasoning

a mathematics unit for high-ability learners in grades 2–4

Spatial Reasoning

The College of William and Mary
School of Education
Center for Gifted Education
P.O. Box 8795
Williamsburg, Virginia 23187

Center for Gifted Education Staff:
Executive Director: Dr. Joyce VanTassel-Baska
Director: Dr. Elissa F. Brown
Curriculum Director: Dr. Kimberley L. Chandler
Curriculum Writer: Dana T. Johnson
Unit Reviewer: Dr. Susan G. Assouline
Research Assistant: Mandy L. Fordham

CENTER FOR GIFTED EDUCATION · THE COLLEGE OF WILLIAM & MARY

Edited by Gretchen Sparling
Production Design by Marjorie Parker

ISBN-13: 978-1-59363-326-4
ISBN-10: 1-59363-326-2

Prufrock Press Inc.
P.O. Box 8813
Waco, TX 76714-8813
Phone: (800) 998-2208
Fax: (800) 240-0333
http://www.prufrock.com

Contents

Part I: Introduction

Part II: Lesson Plans

Part III: Unit Extensions and Resources

Part I: Introduction

Introduction to the Unit

Unit Introduction: *Spatial Reasoning* approaches spatial reasoning through one-dimensional (1-D), two-dimensional (2-D), and three-dimensional (3-D) tasks. Most of the tasks require students to explore representations of three-dimensional objects in two dimensions.

Unit Rationale: All students need to develop good spatial reasoning skills. However, gifted students are more likely to demonstrate an aptitude for advanced spatial reasoning at an early age. They also are more likely to enroll in programs that require advanced math and science knowledge and skills. These courses often serve as a gatekeeper to certain college majors and career opportunities. Because gifted students tend to positively respond to spatial reasoning experiences, they need more of them—both in quantity and complexity—than the standard curriculum provides.

This unit will lay the foundation of spatial reasoning that will prepare students for middle school and beyond. Science courses and higher level mathematics courses require spatial reasoning. Careers in engineering, architecture, medicine, and the sciences, among others, require visualizing relationships that are spatial in nature. Some of these relationships cannot be experienced directly but must be manipulated in the mind. Here are some examples:

- In geometry, to find the diagonal length of a shoebox, you must find the length of a segment that is the hypotenuse of an invisible right triangle.
- In the sciences, molecular structure cannot be observed directly, but the relationships of the atoms need to be understood. Two-dimensional models of these three-dimensional objects often are used.
- The entrance exam for dental school (Dental Admissions Testing, or DAT) has a section called Perceptual Ability that requires interpretation of information about 3-D objects that are given in two dimensions.
- When a surgeon reads an MRI, he or she needs to transfer the collection of two-dimensional images he or she sees into an understanding of a three-dimensional organ or body part.

Spatial skills need to be developed over many years. By beginning in elementary school, students will be better prepared for middle school experiences such as geometry and physical science. This unit builds toward high school and college coursework in mathematics, science, and engineering. This unit is a field-tested tool for developing spatial reasoning ability in students in grades 2–4. These lessons will help develop an aptitude for spatial reasoning that is already present in some students by offering opportunities that correspond to their demonstrated interest and aptitude. The lessons also may be an awakening point for other students who have not had these interests sparked due to lack of prior experiences. This unit will improve spatial reasoning skills of all students who participate.

Differentiation for Gifted Learners: The experiences that are suggested in this unit are intended to be beneficial to all students. However, they are designed with the special needs of gifted students in mind. Reasons to use this unit with gifted learners include the following:

- The regular school curriculum does not provide many experiences necessary to fully develop spatial reasoning skills. This unit provides some of those additional experiences.

- Spatial tasks can provide a level of abstraction that is challenging to gifted learners as they will need to manipulate mental images.
- Ideas are introduced that will support later higher level coursework. For example, high school geometry requires students to recognize congruent figures and their corresponding parts in order to do congruence proofs. The idea of finding volume by slicing is introduced; this is a technique that is used in calculus. Physical sciences require visualizing 3-D structures of things such as atoms and crystals.
- Higher level questions are included in the Extensions section at the end of the unit.
- Written explanations are required, rather than simply giving numerical answers to questions. Writing requires analytical and reflective thinking.
- The task demands are more rigorous than in typical curriculum materials.
- Students are sometimes asked to complete tasks with less teacher support than would be given in a typical math class.
- The vocabulary and language used in student handouts assumes strong verbal skills.
- There is a large amount of mathematical content, which is covered in an accelerated time frame, included in this unit.
- Suggested extension activities allow the unit to be tailored according to the individual abilities of students or needs of a group.
- Much of the work in this unit is inquiry-based. Although this approach may benefit all students, inquiry lessons are an excellent approach to unleash the thinking abilities of gifted students.
- Appropriate problem-solving challenges are posed for mathematically gifted students.

Links to NCTM Standards: NCTM's Principles and Standards for School Mathematics describes spatial reasoning as an important aspect of geometric thinking. Spatial reasoning can provide a way to interpret and describe physical environments and can be a tool in solving problems. The standards propose that students should be able to analyze characteristics and properties of two- and three-dimensional geometric shapes, describe spatial relationships, and apply transformations to analyze mathematical situations.

Suggested Grade Level Range: 2–4

Length of Lessons: Selecting or omitting various activities can adjust the length of the lessons in this unit. A number of the lessons will take more than one 50–60-minute class session. There are many extensions that can be used at other times during the school year for continued work in spatial reasoning.

Timing: Typically, this unit can be completed in 1–2 weeks in a regular classroom setting. Another approach may be to utilize individual lessons throughout the semester. The unit also may be used in a pull-out or enrichment class. Not all lessons need to be included. The teacher may determine the order of the lessons. Table 1 offers teachers suggestions for selecting lessons for various classroom needs.

Extensions: Suggestions for extension activities are included within lessons and at the end of the *Spatial Reasoning* unit. These activities are intended for group and individual use. Teachers also may wish to keep a piece of poster paper hanging in the classroom for students to write questions on while they are working through the unit. Individuals or groups can be selected to research and report back on these questions

Table 1

Suggested Timing for Lessons Depending on Students' Skill Level

Minimum Treatment of This Unit	Intermediate Treatment of This Unit	Maximum Treatment of This Unit
• Younger students (grade 2) • Limited time frame • Students who need more support	• Grade 3 students who are new to this kind of material • Fewer than seven class periods available	• More than seven class periods available • Grade 3 or 4 • Students are very capable
• Lessons 1, 2, 4, 7, and 9 • Be selective about activities within the lessons. Adapt questions as needed. Minimize writing activities for second graders.	• Lessons 1–5, 7, and 9 • Do only the easier extensions.	• All lessons and some extensions. • Assign some independent extensions.
• Trim the pre- and postassessment questions to match what will be covered in the lessons selected.	• Trim the pre- and postassessment questions to match what will be covered in the lessons selected.	• Do all pre- and postassessment questions.

as an additional extension of the unit. The extensions often require students to function somewhat independently. However, you may choose to assign extensions to less-able students by writing scaffold versions of the tasks. The extensions can be used to continue spatial experiences throughout the school year.

Unit Materials

Concrete materials are required to develop spatial reasoning skills. The following materials are referenced in the unit and are available at many educational supply outlets. Teacher-made materials often can be used as alternatives.

- **Polydrons™:** These are a set of plastic polygons that can be snapped together to make polyhedra. The same company makes similar materials that have hollow interiors of the polygons and are marketed as Polydron Frameworks™.
- **Miras:** These are clear red plastic devices that have reflective properties and are used to draw symmetric images. They are similar to mirrors but images can be seen through the plastic.
- **Patty paper:** This paper comes in a large package of small square sheets. The paper looks like waxed paper but is more transparent and easier to write on. It gets its name from the fact that its main purpose is for restaurants to put between raw hamburger patties. You might ask your cafeteria manager to help you find a source for this, or you can order it from Key Curriculum Press at http://www.keypress.com.
- **Play dough:** See the end of Lesson 7 for a recipe.

- **D-stix**: These color-coded plastic rods and multipronged plastic connectors can be used to create basic polyhedrons, structures in solid geometry, or advanced three-dimensional geometric designs. They are available from educational supply houses such as ETA/Cuisenaire.
- **Zome products:** These are plastic rods and balls that are joined to create 3-D structures. They are available from a number of vendors but they sell their own products at http://www.zometool.com.

Assessment

Each lesson has suggested assessments but teachers may use additional methods to determine student understanding.

Math Journals: A suggested method is students' use of math journals. If students maintain a math journal, they can be asked to solve a single problem in their journal and explain their reasoning. Teachers may then collect these journals at the end of each lesson and grade students' recorded responses.

Preassessment: This is not a readiness test. It is intended to give you a baseline indicator of what students know before they start the unit. Typically, students will not do well on the preassessment. If some students perform well on the preassessment, you should use the unit extensions to extend and challenge their learning.

Postassessment: This is included at the end of the unit. It is parallel in structure to the preassessment. If you administer both instruments, you will be able to tell if students learned the concepts as a result of participating in this unit.

Unit Glossary

Congruent: Having exactly the same size and shape. Congruent polygons have corresponding angles that are congruent and corresponding sides that are congruent.

Cube: A solid figure in which every face is a square and every edge is the same length.

Domino: A polygon made from two squares that meet with full edges touching.

Edge: The line segment where two faces of a polyhedron intersect each other.

Ellipse: Essentially a stretched circle. (Formally, it is the cross section of a cone that is obtained by slicing the cone with a slice that is not parallel to a side of the cone or the base.)

Face: A plane figure that serves as one side of a solid figure. The face of a polyhedron is a polygon.

Glide reflection: A symmetry transformation that is made up of two other symmetry transformations, a translation and a reflection.

Line: A set of points that form a straight path extending infinitely in two directions. Lines are often called *straight lines* to distinguish them from curves, which are often called *curved lines*. Part of a line with two endpoints is called a *line segment*.

Parallel lines: Lines lying in the same plane that are always the same distance apart.

Parallelogram: A quadrilateral with both pairs of opposite sides parallel.

Pentomino: A polygon made from five squares that meet with full edges touching.

Plane: A flat surface containing all of the straight lines that connect any two points on it.

Point: A location in space.

Polygon: A simple (no lines intersect except at vertices), closed, plane figure bounded by straight sides.

Polyhedron: A solid figure bounded by flat faces. Plural is *polyhedra* or *polyhedrons*.

Polyominoes: Polygons made from any number of squares that meet with full edges touching.

Prism: A solid figure having bases or ends that are parallel, congruent polygons, and sides that are rectangles or other parallelograms.

Projection: In this unit, a projection is made of a solid (3-dimensional) object onto a plane (2-dimensional surface). The image or shadow of the object is the projection. You also may project a 2-dimensional object onto a line. Thus, a projection removes one dimension from the original object or image.

Pyramid: A polyhedron with any polygon for its base. The other faces are triangles that meet at a point or vertex.

Quadrilateral: A polygon with four sides.

Reflection (flip): To reflect an object means to produce its mirror image. Every reflection has a mirror line. This transformation requires the figure to move out of the plane, through space, and back onto the plane as it flips over the mirror line.

Rotation (turn): To rotate a figure means to turn it about a point on the figure. The direction of the turn can be given as clockwise or counterclockwise. The magnitude of the turn can be given in degrees (such as 90 degrees) or a fraction of a full circle (such as a ¼ turn). The figure formed by this procedure is a rotation.

Similar figures: Figures with the same shape but not necessarily the same size. The angle measures are the same but side lengths are not necessarily the same length.

Symmetric or symmetrical: A figure is symmetrical if the two images on opposite sides of a line are mirror images.

Tetromino: A polygon made from four squares that meet with full edges touching.

Translation (slide): To translate a figure means to move it within a plane without reflecting or rotating it. A translation has a direction (such as right, left, up, down) and a distance (units can be represented on grid paper).

Trapezoid: A quadrilateral with one pair of parallel sides.

Triomino: A polygon made from three squares that meet with full edges touching.

Vertex: A corner point of a geometric figure. The plural is *vertices*. In a two-dimensional figure, it is the point where two line segments meet. In a three-dimensional figure, it is the point where three or more faces meet.

Part II: Lesson Plans

Lesson Plans

Lesson 1: Preassessment

Instructional Purpose

- To assess student knowledge and understanding of unit topics

Materials and Handouts

- Preassessment (Handout 1A)
- Preassessment Answer Key (Teacher Resource 1)

Activities

1. Explain to students that they will be beginning a new unit of study focused on spatial reasoning. Tell students that in order to get a good sense of how much they already know and to be able to tell how much they have learned by the end of the unit, they will need to take a preassessment. Distribute the **Preassessment (Handout 1A)** and have students complete it individually.

2. Collect and score the preassessment using the **Preassessment Answer Key (Teacher Resource 1)**.

3. Have students discuss which aspects of the preassessment they found difficult. Explain that throughout the unit they will be thinking about challenging questions that relate to concepts on the preassessment.

Notes to Teacher

1. The preassessment given in this unit serves multiple purposes. Performance on the preassessment should establish a baseline against which performance on the postassessment may be compared. In addition, teachers may use information obtained from the preassessment to aid instructional planning, as strengths and areas for improvement among students become apparent.

2. Students should have a unit notebook and folder that they can use throughout the unit to respond to Math Journal questions, other written assignments, and to keep any handouts from the unit. The notebook also can hold a running list of unit vocabulary, which should be displayed in the classroom in chart form.

Assessment

- Preassessment

Preassessment (Handout 1A)

Directions: Do your best to answer the following questions.

1. One or more of the figures below can be turned (not flipped over) to look like Figure A at the right. Circle the figure(s) below that can be turned to look like Figure A.

Figure A

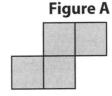

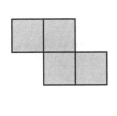
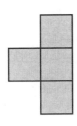
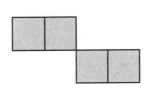

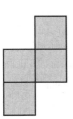
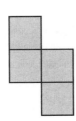
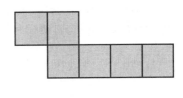

2. Draw all lines of symmetry on this figure.

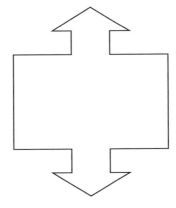

3. Is the figure in Question 2 a polygon? Why or why not?_____

_____

_____

_____

4. Draw the mirror image of this figure over the line.

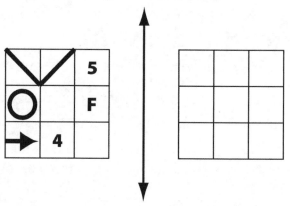

5. How many dimensions does a triangle have? _____

6. How many dimensions does a can of soup have? _____

7. Look at the pattern drawn below.

   a. If you cut out this pattern and folded on the dotted lines to form a box, would the box have a top? _____

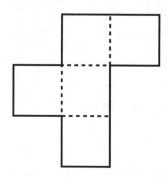

   b. Put an **X** on the square that is the bottom of the box.

8. How many cubes are needed to make the building below? _____

   How do you know? _____

   _____

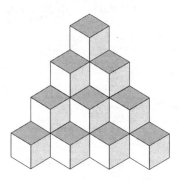

9. Mrs. Smith put a can of soda on the overhead projector and turned the lamp on. What could the shadow on the screen look like? Draw it.

10. If you cut a hot dog like the picture below, what would the cross section look like?

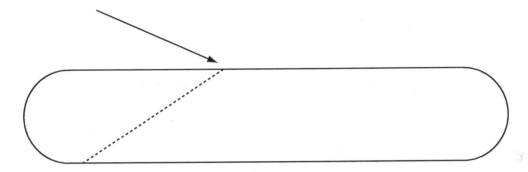

    Choose the best picture from below:

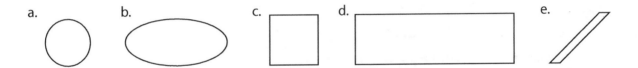

Preassessment Answer Key
(Teacher Resource 1)

Directions: Do your best to answer the following questions.

1. One or more of the figures below can be turned (not flipped over) to look like Figure A at the right. Circle the figure(s) below that can be turned to look like Figure A.

Figure A

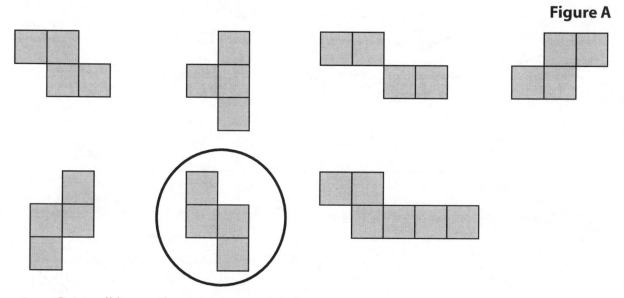

2. Draw all lines of symmetry on this figure.

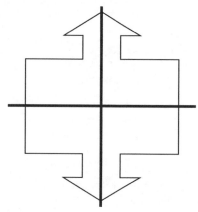

3. Is the figure in Question 2 a polygon? Why or why not?

Yes, it is a flat (lies in a plane), closed figure made of straight lines. No lines cross except at the endpoints.

4.   Draw the mirror image of this figure over the line.

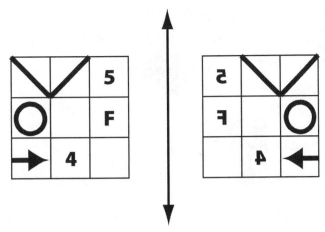

5.   How many dimensions does a triangle have? **2**

6.   How many dimensions does a can of soup have? **3**

7.   Look at the pattern drawn below.

   a. If you cut out this pattern and folded on the dotted lines to form a box, would the box have a top? **No.**

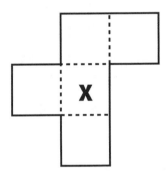

   b. Put an **X** on the square that is the bottom of the box.

8.   How many cubes are needed to make the building below? **20**

   How do you know?

   Students may write the number in each tower or the number in each layer and add them up. Any reasonable explanation is acceptable.

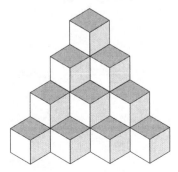

9. Mrs. Smith put a can of soda on the overhead projector and turned the lamp on. What could the shadow on the screen look like? Draw it.

    The usual upright position =

    Lying on its side =

10. If you cut a hot dog like the picture below, what would the cross section look like?

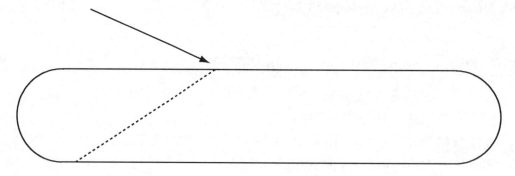

    Choose the best picture from below:

a. 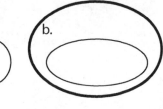 b. c. d. e.

Lesson 2: Introduction to Dimensions

Instructional Purpose

- To introduce the idea of dimensions
- To demonstrate the advantage of information gained by larger numbers of dimensions available to our perceptions
- To build geometric solids and identify the 0-, 1-, and 2-dimensional characteristics of the solid

Materials and Handouts

- Frogs (one frog per student; Handout 2A)
- Model of Dimensions (Teacher Resource 1)
- Dimensions (Handout 2B)
- Dimensions Answer Key (Teacher Resource 2)
- 1-inch square tiles or paper squares (about six per student)
- A pop-up children's book
- Toothpicks and gumdrops, marshmallows, clay or Play dough, or commercially available materials for building polyhedra
- One small cube (1-inch cube or larger is best) for each student

Vocabulary

Line: A set of points that form a straight path extending infinitely in two directions. Lines often are called *straight lines* to distinguish them from curves, which are often called *curved lines*. Part of a line with two endpoints is called a *line segment*.

Plane: A flat surface containing all of the straight lines that connect any two points on it.

Point: A location in space.

Polyhedron: A solid figure bounded by flat faces. Plural is *polyhedra* or *polyhedrons*.

Prism: A solid figure having bases or ends that are parallel, congruent polygons, and sides that are rectangles or other parallelograms.

Vertex: A corner point of a geometric figure. The plural is *vertices*. In a 2-dimensional figure, it is the point where two line segments meet. In a 3-dimensional figure, it is the point where 3 or more faces meet.

Activities

1. Introduce the idea of dimensions by drawing a long line across the chalkboard. Welcome students to Lineland and give each student small paper **Frogs (Handout 2A).** Ask students to imagine that one of the frogs lives in Lineland. He cannot go anywhere else except move along the line. Have a student come to the board and demonstrate how the frog would move in Lineland. (Forward and backward; no jumping off the board or moving off the line).

2. Have frogs move to Flatland by using a tabletop in the classroom. Use the following questions to have a discussion with students.
    - How do the frogs move in Flatland? (No jumping, but they may move forward, backward, or sideways.)

- What do the paper frogs of Flatland look like when they see each other? Encourage students to stoop so their eyes are level with the tabletop. (The frogs look like a line segment as only the edge of the paper can be seen by other frogs in this flat environment.)
- What are advantages of Flatland over Lineland? (More directions to move.) What are the constraints? (They cannot jump over each other; only sliding around is permitted.)

3. Move the frogs to Spaceland, which is represented by the classroom. Discuss the similarities of the different lands and the advantages of Spaceland. In all of the lands, the frogs can move forward or backward. In Flatland, they can get around each other. But, they have the most mobility in Spaceland where they can jump up into the air and over each other, in any direction.

4. Introduce the term *dimension* using the following definitions and connect back to the three lands.
   - **0-D:** A point is a location in space. It has no dimensions.
   - **1-D:** A line is a set of points that form a straight path extending infinitely in two directions. A line segment is a part of a line with two endpoints. In everyday speech, lines often are called straight lines to distinguish them from curves, which are often called curved lines. In this unit, a line means a straight line.
   - **2-D:** A plane is a flat surface extending infinitely in all directions. All 2-D objects lie in a plane. For example, a rectangle is a two-dimensional figure. Two numbers (generally called length and width) are required to determine it.
   - **3-D:** Space. Movement may occur in all directions. A cube is a three-dimensional figure. Three numbers (generally length, width, and height) are necessary to describe its dimensions.

5. Use the projection screen in your classroom as an example of the different dimensions. Indicate that the roller represents a line; that is a 1-D figure. Pull down the screen and ask students how many dimensions the screen represents. (2-D.) Tell students that if you could create a box popping out from the screen, it would represent a 3-D object.

6. Use parked cars as another example of the different dimensions. A single car can be thought of as a large point (0-D). When cars parallel park next to a curb along the street, you can think of this as one-dimensional parking (points extended in one direction). A parking lot can be thought of as a 2-D object (points extended over a plane). A parking garage is a 3-D parking arrangement because it extends the 2-D parking lot in one more direction.

7. Ask students to find objects in the room that are examples of 1-D, 2-D, and 3-D items. For example, the line between tiles on the floor (1-D), the tiles on the floor (2-D), and a desk (3-D).

8. Give students 1-inch tiles. Tell students to think of them as very large points. On the overhead projector, place one tile and add to it in one direction. Have them copy your line of tiles at their desks. Ask students in how many directions are they adding tiles. (One.) Explain to students that this represents one dimension.

9. Make a rectangle of tiles on the overhead projector and have students do the same. Ask students how many dimensions are represented. (Two.)

10. Have students make a 2 x 3 rectangle with tiles and then build upward on the base. Ask students how many dimensions are represented. (Three.)

11. Show students the **Model of Dimensions (Teacher Resource 1)**. Use the point to represent zero dimensions, the line to illustrate one dimension, the rectangle to illustrate two dimensions, and the pop-up figure to illustrate three dimensions.

12. Show students a pop-up book and discuss why this technique is effective in a storybook. Use the following questions to lead a class discussion. Time permitting, you may want to let students design and make their own pop-up pictures.
    - Why does the author use the pop-up image?
    - Would you prefer to read a pop-up version of a picture book or a version with only pictures drawn on the 2-D pages? Why?
    - When you see 2-D pictures in a book, can you imagine the 3-D objects that are shown?
    - Why do you think a 2-D picture is sufficient to make us understand what the 3-D object is?

13. Distribute materials to create models with Zometools, toothpicks and gumdrops, marshmallows, clay, or play dough. Have students make a triangle. Ask students how many dimensions the triangle has. Have students make a second triangle the same size and shape as the first. Then they should connect the two triangles to make a prism (see Figure 1). Identify vertices (corners), edges, faces, and the polyhedron. Ask students how many dimensions are needed for each of these characteristics. (0, 1, 2, and 3.) Tell students that a solid figure bounded by flat faces is called a polyhedron.

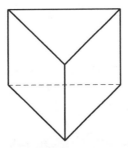

Figure 1. Example of polyhedron.

14. Use the following questions to have students discuss in pairs and then as a whole group. Encourage students to ask their parents if they can look at the map next time they go on a car trip; this is a good spatial activity.
    - How many dimensions does a map have?
    - Why do you think maps are not made to be 3-D?
    - Has anyone had the experience of riding in the car in a hilly area where you were surprised because the map made the road look flat?

15. Distribute **Dimensions (Handout 2B)** and have students complete it. Assess student responses with the **Dimensions Answer Key (Teacher Resource 2)**.

16. Close the lesson by reminding students that this mathematics unit is about spatial reasoning, which is the ability to understand movement or change in images or objects within any number of dimensions or movement between dimensions.

Notes to Teacher

1. This unit represents a point with a dot so that the point is visible, but the point has no length, width, or height. Students may argue that points have very minute length and width measurements. However, teachers need to reinforce the idea that it is not the representation, but the definition that determines what a point is. A point is a location in space, and has no dimensions.

2. Euclid, a Greek mathematician who lived about 325 B.C.–265 B.C. and is often called the father of geometry, gave the vague definition of a point as "that which has no part."

3. It is difficult to say that any real-world object is one-dimensional, as the width of the object is greater than a point. Even a line drawn on paper has width greater than a point. But, we think of items such as spaghetti as being one-dimensional objects as the width is negligible. The distinction between two and three dimensions is the most relevant for functioning in the real world. Therefore, this unit will concentrate on two and three dimensions and movement between those two dimensions.

4. You may use commercially available materials such as Zome products or D-stix, to build the three-dimensional solids in this lesson.

5. Students may have trouble with the idea that a vertex of a polyhedron is a point. Teachers can demonstrate this concept if they use marshmallows and toothpicks as building materials. The marshmallows are used as the vertices of polygons and polyhedra. Whenever you join two toothpicks, the intersection is a point and is represented by a marshmallow.

6. Be aware of student confusion of the following terms in this unit. When using each term in context, it helps to write the word on the board so that students get a visual cue for the distinctions in the words.
   * **polygon:** 2-D figure,
   * **polyhedron:** a 3-D figure such as those that were constructed in this lesson, and
   * **Polydrons™:** commercially distributed plastic polygons that snap together to build polyhedrons. (List this word if only you are using these materials.)

7. For an elaborate example of a pop-up book, look for one illustrated by Robert Sabuda. One example is *Alice's Adventures in Wonderland*.

8. Food items such as M&M's, Cheerios, and raisins, can be used instead of tiles to illustrate dimensions. However, be aware that use of candy can distract students from the substance of the concepts. You can reinforce the ideas of dimensions by talking about M&M's as being big points and therefore 0-D, licorice strings as a 1-D candy, Fruit Roll-ups as 2-D, and a cake as 3-D (especially if it is a rectangular cake, you can measure the three dimensions: length, width, and height).

Assessment

- Dimensions (Handout 2B)

Extensions

The following student activities can be used to extend the lesson.

1. Have students build any polyhedron they like with Polydrons™. (See the Unit Materials section in the Introduction to the Unit for a recommended source for purchasing these plastic materials.) Have each child present his or her structure with an explanation of how many vertices, edges, and faces it has. Take digital photos of their creations. Ask students how many dimensions the picture has and how many dimensions are represented in the complete structure.

2. Have students make a pattern with colored tiles by adding tiles in the direction of one dimension. They should use three colors and have a classmate continue the pattern.

3. Ask each student to make a pattern with colored tiles in two dimensions using three colors and have a classmate continue the pattern.

4. Have students make a pattern with colored cubes in three dimensions. Have them use two colors and have a classmate continue the pattern.

5. Read *Flat Stanley* by Jeff Brown and Scott Nash. Stanley experiences life as a two-dimensional figure in a three-dimensional world. Discuss the advantages and disadvantages of being 3-D or 2-D in Stanley's situation.

6. Bring in a 3-D Tic-Tac-Toe game. Have students play and compare it to the usual two-dimensional version.

7. Have students act as points. Tell them to imagine that they are a point living in 0 dimensions. Have students demonstrate how they can move in 0 dimensions. Repeat for 1, 2, and 3 dimensions.

Frogs (Handout 2A)

Model of Dimensions (Teacher Resource 1)

1.

•   How many dimensions? _____

_____   How many dimensions? _____

   How many dimensions? _____

2.   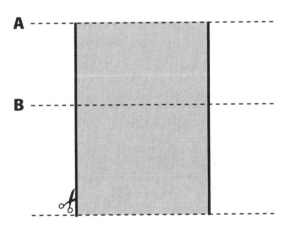

A -   Make a valley fold along line A.

B -   Make a mountain fold on this line, cut on the 2 solid lines, pop up the shaded rectangle, and reverse the crease on the white part of the paper along line B to make the dotted line into a valley fold.

-   Make a valley fold on this line.

How many dimensions are represented by the pop-up figure? _____

Dimensions (Handout 2B)

1. How many dimensions are represented by each of these?

    a. A crack in the sidewalk where two squares are joined _____

    b. A picture of a car _____

    c. A paper cup _____

2. Your teacher will give you a cube to use to answer these questions.

    a. How many vertices (corners) does the cube have? _____

       How many dimensions does the corner represent? _____

    b. How many edges does the cube have? _____

       How many dimensions are represented by an edge? _____

    c. How many square faces does the cube have? _____

       How many dimensions does a square face represent? _____

    d. Circle the best answer. A cube is an example of:
       i.   A one-dimensional object
       ii. A two-dimensional object
       iii. A three-dimensional object

Dimensions Answer Key
(Teacher Resource 2)

1. How many dimensions are represented by each of these?

    a. A crack in the sidewalk where 2 squares are joined **1**

    b. A picture of a car **2**

    c. A paper cup **3**

2. Your teacher will give you a cube to use to answer these questions.

    a. How many vertices (corners) does the cube have? **8**

        How many dimensions does the corner represent? **0**

    b. How many edges does the cube have? **12**

        How many dimensions are represented by an edge? **1**

    c. How many square faces does the cube have? **6**

        How many dimensions does a square face represent? **2**

    d. Circle the best answer. A cube is an example of:

        iii.   A three-dimensional object

Lesson 3: Slides, Flips, Turns, and Glides

Instructional Purpose

- To recognize and create geometric transformations (translations, rotations, reflections, and glide reflections)

Materials and Handouts

- L-Shape (Handout 3A)
- Transformations (Handout 3B)
- Transformations Practice (Handout 3C)
- Name It! (Handout 3D)
- Name It! Answer Key (Teacher Resource 1)
- Transformations Assessment (Handout 3E)
- Transformations Assessment Answer Key (Teacher Resource 2)
- Overhead spinner (optional)
- Patty paper

Vocabulary

Glide reflection: A symmetry transformation that is made up of two other symmetry transformations, a translation and a reflection.

Reflection (flip): To reflect an object means to produce its mirror image. Every reflection has a mirror line. This transformation requires the figure to move out of the plane, through space, and back onto the plane as it flips over the mirror line.

Rotation (turn): To rotate a figure means to turn it about a point on the figure. The direction of the turn can be given as clockwise or counterclockwise. The magnitude of the turn can be given in degrees (such as 90 degrees) or a fraction of a full circle (such as a ¼ turn). The figure formed by this procedure is a rotation.

Translation (slide): To translate a figure means to move it within a plane without reflecting or rotating it. A translation has a direction (such as right, left, up, down) and a distance (units can be represented on grid paper).

Activities

1. Remind students about Flatland that was used introduced in Lesson 2 and represented by a tabletop. Discuss as a class how the inhabitants of Flatland move around. (Slides and turns.) Explain to students that the mathematical names for these moves are *translations* and *rotations*.

2. Distribute **L-Shape (Handout 3A)** and display a transparency copy on the overhead projector. Have students cut out the L-shape at the bottom of the page. Demonstrate the translation and rotation of L for the class. Have students practice translating and rotating by giving the following instructions. Model on the overhead how to move the L-shape.
   - Translation: Trace the original position of the L-shape with an overhead pen so that students can compare the result to the original. Slide the L-shape to a new position anywhere on the grid without turning it. Ask students how the new image compares to the original. (It looks the same but is moved to a new location.)

- Rotation: Keep one of the vertices fixed and turn the L-shape around the point ¼ turn clockwise, that another ¼ turn, and so forth. Explain to students that this movement is similar to how hands move on a clock. An overhead spinner can be used to demonstrate how the hand rotates around the center. Ask students if L-shapes in Flatland can translate and rotate. (Yes; these are the only two ways it can move.)

3. Explain to students that you are going to demonstrate two different transformations that require the availability of a third dimension. Demonstrate the following to the class.
    - Reflection: Flip the figure over the horizontal line (the x-axis). The result is a mirror image of the shape you flipped. Trace the L-shape with an overhead pen before you flip it so that students can compare the original to the reflected image. Flip the image again over the vertical line (the y-axis). Ask students if the resulting image would look the same if they flipped over the y-axis first and then the x-axis. (Yes.)
    - Glide reflection: Slide the L-shape to the right and then flip it over the x-axis. Another variation is to slide down and then flip over the y-axis. (The key is to slide in the direction of the axis that you will flip over.)

4. Distribute **Transformations (Handout 3B)** and connect the definitions to the movements students just practiced.

5. Choose individual students to demonstrate moving the L-shape on the overhead projector and have the rest of the class assess whether he or she is correct. Use the following suggestions or make up your own.
    - Translate the shape two units down.
    - Rotate around the points A, B, or C.
        o Rotate ¼ turn counterclockwise around point A.
        o Rotate ½ turn clockwise around point A.
    - Reflect the shape over a horizontal line.
    - Show a glide reflection that translates the shape upward and reflected over the y-axis.

6. Have students place the L on the axes so that the letter A sits at the origin as shown in Figure 2.

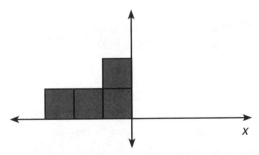

Figure 2. Example of x-axis with L-shape.

7. Have students predict what the image would look like if they rotate the shape ¼ turn clockwise using point A as the pivot point. They should lightly shade their prediction on their handout with a pencil. Rotate the shape and check to see if their predictions were correct. Label the image A.

8. Repeat the procedure except use point B as the pivot point for the rotation. Label the result B.

9. Repeat the procedure again except use point C as the pivot point for the rotation. Label the result C.

10. Discuss how the image is different if the pivot point of the rotation changes. The three images should look like in Figure 3:

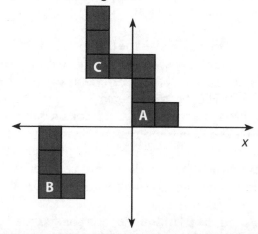

Figure 3. Example of x-axis showing rotation changes.

11. On the board, draw the vertical line and image shown in Figure 4. Have students copy it in their math journals and demonstrate a glide reflection.

Figure 4. Example of vertical line image for display.

12. Distribute **Transformations Practice (Handout 3C)** and have students complete it in small groups. Students may use patty paper to trace the images and help them solve the problems if needed. Discuss the answers as a class.

13. Distribute **Name It! (Handout 3D)** and have students complete the activity. Tell students that other transformations are possible so they must be able to justify their answers. Discuss their results as a class. Use the **Name It! Answer Key (Teacher Resource 1)** for assessment.

14. Distribute **Transformations Assessment (Handout 3E)** and have students complete the activity individually. Use the Assessment **Answer Key (Teacher Resource 2)** for grading.

Math Journal

Have students write a response to this prompt in their math journals:
- Write about an example of transformations in everyday life. Describe the situation and identify the type of transformation. Some examples are: pushing in a chair at the table, patterns on wallpaper, fabric prints, or quilt patterns.

Notes to Teacher

1. Glide reflections can first be glided then reflected or reflected then glided. The order does not affect the resulting image. However, it is easier for students to understand the orders given in the term glide reflection—glide, then reflect. The key is to slide in the direction of the mirror line and flip over the mirror line.

2. Here is a summary of transformations:

    Translation (slide): To translate a figure means to move it within a plane without reflecting or rotating it. A translation has a direction (such as right, left, up, down) and a distance (on grid paper you can say how many units).

    Rotation (turn): To rotate a figure means to turn it about a point on the figure. The direction of the turn can be given as clockwise or counterclockwise. The magnitude of the turn can be given in degrees (such as 90 degrees) or a fraction of a full circle (such as a ¼ turn).

    Reflection (flip): To reflect an object means to produce its mirror image. Every reflection has a mirror line. This transformation requires the figure to move out of the plane, through space, and back onto the plane.

    Glide Reflection: This transformation is a combination of two of the transformations given above. It is the result of a translation in the direction of the mirror line and a reflection over the mirror line (or reflection and then translation). Note: The direction of the slide is perpendicular to the direction of the flip.

    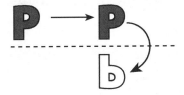

Assessment

- Transformations Practice (Handout 3C)
- Name It! (Handout 3D)
- Transformations Assessment (Handout 3E)
- Math Journal entries

Extensions

The following student activities can be used to extend the lesson.

1. Have students play Tetris online at a number of Web sites or on a hand-held game player. An example of a Web site that offers virtual Tetris games is:
   - http://www.surfnetkids.com/games/tetris.htm

   Explain to students that the prefix *tetra* means four and all of the pieces in the game are tetraminoes. After playing the game, students should be able to identify transformations that are used in Tetris.

2. Ask students to write about the relationship between the term *translate* (as used in this lesson) and the term *translate* meaning to change into a different language. How are the two similar?

3. Tell students to create a design on a geoboard so that:
   - When it is rotated by ½ turn, it looks the same as the original.
   - When it is rotated ¼ turn, it looks the same as the original.
   - When it is reflected over a vertical line, it looks the same but when reflected over a horizontal line, it does not look the same.
   - When it is reflected over a vertical line, it looks the same and when reflected over horizontal line, it looks the same.

4. If you have access to a computer lab, have students try the game Logo on a computer. Teachers may download a free program at http://www.softronix.com/logo.html. This software allows students to direct the movements of a "turtle" by using rotations and translations. You also may use a logo-based virtual program called Turtle Pond at http://illuminations.nctm.org/ActivityDetail.aspx?ID=83.

5. Have students draw a pair of x and y coordinate axes on an index card. Print a capital letter in the upper left corner of each quadrant. Have students draw the reflection over a vertical line, horizontal line, or rotated.

6. Encourage students to determine if it matters whether you translate or reflect first in a glide reflection.

7. Bring in some wallpaper samples and have students identify transformations in some of the samples. You may see some mathematical examples of wallpaper at http://www.clarku.edu/~djoyce/wallpaper.

8. Draw a question mark (or the flag shown in Figure 5) on the board. Have students copy it on the center of a piece of copy paper. Then give directions orally as follows and have students draw the result for each step.
   a. Slide the figure to the right and label it A. Is this a translation, rotation, reflection, or glide reflection?

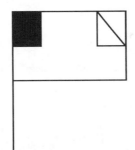

Figure 5. Example of flag for transformation exercise.

    b. Draw a horizontal line under the figure. Flip the figure over the line. Is this a translation, rotation, reflection, or glide reflection?

    c. Flip the original figure over the horizontal line and slide to the left. Is this a translation, rotation, reflection, or glide reflection?

    d. Turn the original figure ¼ turn clockwise. Is this a translation, rotation, reflection, or glide reflection?

9. Have students draw reflections of all of the letters of the alphabet and the digits 0–9. Discuss which letters look the same when reflected.

10. Find pictures done by the artist M. C. Escher that use translations, rotations, and reflections. Ask students to identify these transformations in the pieces of art. Check the library for a book of Escher prints or visit a Web site, such as http://www.mcescher.com.

11. Have a pair of students stand at the front of the room facing the class. Give directions of simple movements such as, "Put your hand on the top of your head," "Put your hand on your hip," or "Put your finger on your nose." Have one student do the moves with the left hand and foot while the other does the moves with their right hand and foot. Ask the class to describe the movements in terms of transformations. They should be reflections of each other. Students may design their own movements to carry out with a partner, all in form of reflections.

L-Shape (Handout 3A)

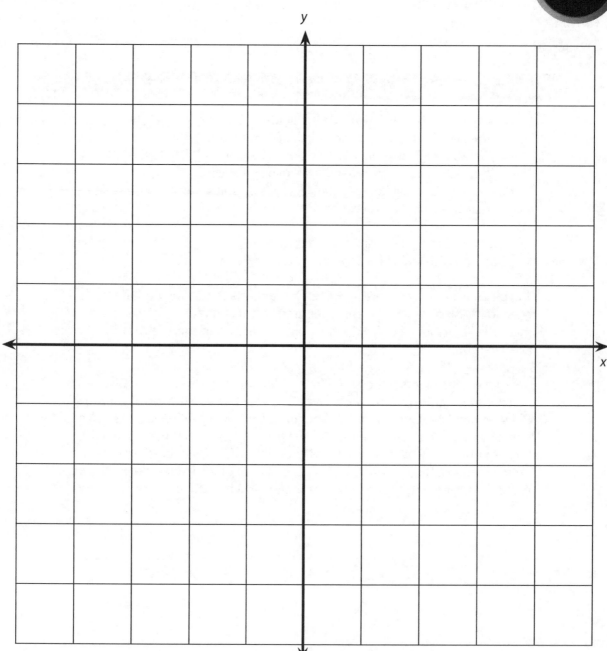

Name_____ Date_____

Translation (slide)

Rotation (turn)

Reflection (flip)

Glide reflection

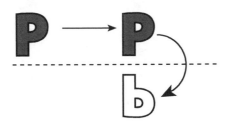

Transformations Practice (Handout 3C)

On this grid, one unit of length is the distance between two dots horizontally or vertically. Draw the shape after the transformation.

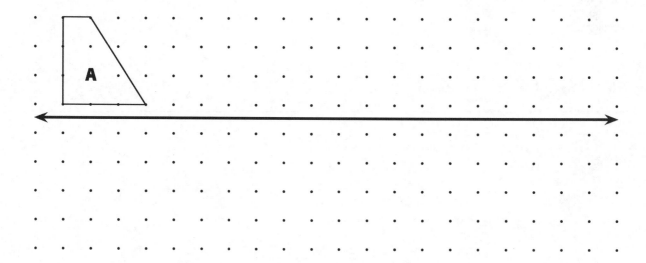

1. Translate polygon A by moving it 5 units down, trace it, and label it B.

2. Go back to polygon A. Use a glide reflection to move figure A by translating 10 units to the right, trace it, and then reflect it over the given line. Label the result C.

3. Rotate the figure below ¼ turn clockwise around point B and draw the result. Use tracing paper if you wish.

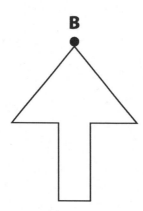

4. Rotate the figure below ¼ turn clockwise around point C and draw the result. Use tracing paper if you wish.

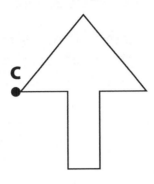

5. Draw any figure on the left side of the line. Then draw what it looks like if it is reflected over the given line.

Name It! (Handout 3D)

Directions: Circle the name of the transformation that changes the figure on the left to the one on the right. It might take more than one transformation and there may be more than one correct answer! The first one is completed for you.

1.

（Translation）   Rotation   Reflection   Glide Reflection

2.

Translation   Rotation   Reflection   Glide Reflection

3.

Translation   Rotation   Reflection   Glide Reflection

4.

Translation   Rotation   Reflection   Glide Reflection

5.

Translation   Rotation   Reflection   Glide Reflection

6.

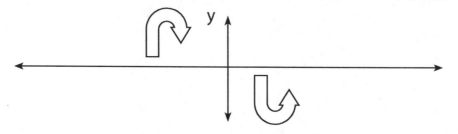

Translation   Rotation   Reflection   Glide Reflection

Name It! Answer Key (Teacher Resource 1)

Directions: Circle the name of the transformation that changes the figure on the left to the one on the right. It might take more than one transformation and there may be more than one correct answer! The first one is completed for you.

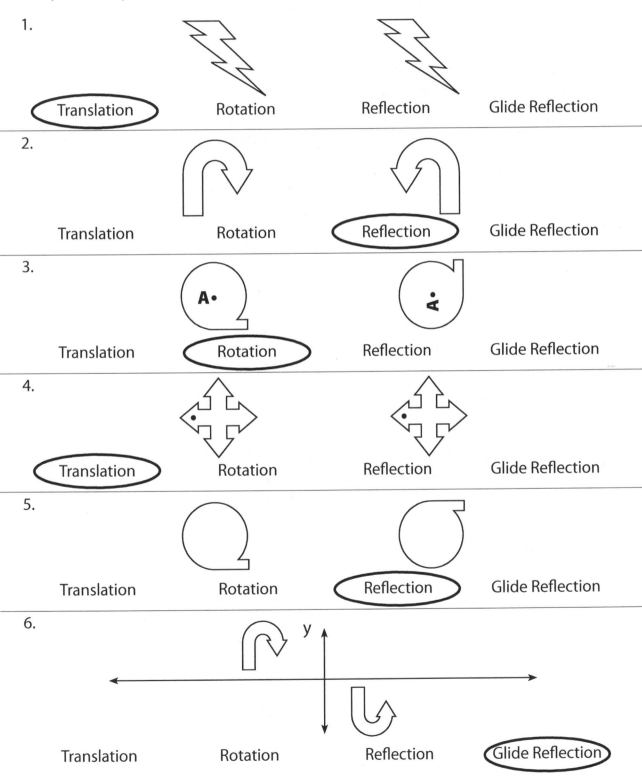

1.

(Translation) Rotation Reflection Glide Reflection

2.

Translation Rotation (Reflection) Glide Reflection

3.

Translation (Rotation) Reflection Glide Reflection

4.

(Translation) Rotation Reflection Glide Reflection

5.

Translation Rotation (Reflection) Glide Reflection

6.

Translation Rotation Reflection (Glide Reflection)

Transformations Assessment (Handout 3E)

Directions: Describe the transformation(s) needed to move the items in these stories. Circle the correct answer.

1. Neal wants to move the picture that is hanging on the wall. What transformation does he use to move it? Choose the best answer.

    a. Move it directly to the right
       i. Translation
       ii. Reflection
       iii. Rotation

    b. Move it up a little bit
       i. Translation
       ii. Reflection
       iii. Rotation

2. Martha says she does not like the picture at all! So she turns it over and hangs it back at the same height on a nail on the right side of the wall. The back of the picture is now showing. What transformation did she use?
    a. Translation
    b. Reflection
    c. Rotation

3. Maria is moving the furniture in her living room. She wants to move the sofa to the middle of the opposite wall in the room shown below. Describe the transformations she is likely to use to move it there.

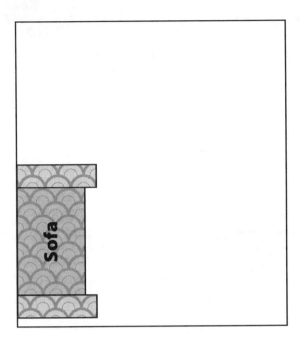

4. Describe the transformation(s) that create this footprint pattern. Choose the best answer. Under the picture, explain your answer.

   a. Translation
   b. Reflection
   c. Rotation
   d. Glide reflection

Transformations Assessment Answer Key (Teacher Resource 2)

Directions: Describe the transformation(s) needed to move the items in these stories. Circle the correct answer.

1. Neal wants to move the picture that is hanging on the wall. What transformation does he use to move it? Choose the best answer.

   a. Move it directly to the right
      i. Translation

   b. Move it up a little bit
      i. Translation

2. Martha says she does not like the picture at all! So she turns it over and hangs it back at the same height on a nail on the right side of the wall. The back of the picture is now showing. What transformation did she use?
      b. Reflection

3. Maria is moving the furniture in her living room. She wants to move the sofa to the middle of the opposite wall in the room shown below. Describe the transformations she is likely to use to move it there.

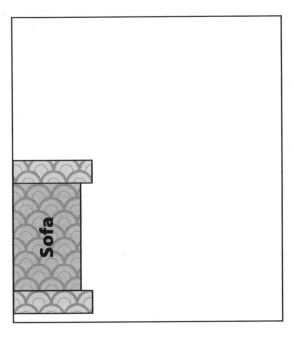

One possible answer: She might pull it out from the wall (translation). Then rotate it ½ turn either to the right or left (rotation). Then push it against the wall. If the placement is not exactly the middle of the wall, she can slide it into place (translation). Note: Students should use a cut-out of the sofa to demonstrate their reasoning if there is any question.

4. Describe the transformation(s) that create this footprint pattern. Choose the best answer. Under the picture, explain your answer.

     a. Translation

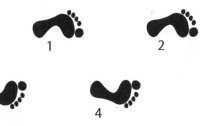

Possibilities:

- **Footprints 1 and 3 move forward (translations).**

- **Footprint 3 moves forward and then is reflected over an imaginary horizontal line to make footprint 1 (glide reflection). Footprint 4 prints footprint 2 via a glide reflection.**

- **Using footprints 1 and 2 as a unit, they can be reflected over a horizontal line to obtain footprints 3 and 4.**

Lesson 4: Reflections and Symmetry

Instructional Purpose

- To learn about line symmetry

Materials and Handouts

- Letter Symmetry (Handout 4A)
- Lines of Symmetry (Handout 4B)
- Lines of Symmetry Answer Key (Teacher Resource 1)
- Two Kinds of Line Symmetry (Teacher Resource 2)
- Geoboards (Handout 4D)
- Home Reflections (Handout 4E)
- Drawing Reflections (Handout 4F)
- Mirror Reflections (Handout 4G)
- Mirror Reflections Answer Key (Teacher Resource 3)
- Reflective Writing (Handout 4H; overhead copy for teacher)
- Miras
- Geoboards, one per student (and overhead geoboard for teacher)
- Rubber bands for geoboards
- Scissors
- Twenty 1-inch cubes per student
- Rulers (one per pair of students)
- Patty paper
- Scrap paper

Vocabulary

Congruent: Having exactly the same size and shape. Congruent polygons have corresponding angles that are congruent and corresponding sides that are congruent.

Symmetric: A figure is symmetrical if the two images on opposite sides of a line are mirror images.

Activities

1. Distribute geoboards to every student and have them create a design with rubber bands. Ask them to show their designs.

2. Ask students to try and divide their geoboard design into two equal parts with a rubber band, making the parts mirror images of each other. Explain that this is called a *line of symmetry* or it could be called a *mirror line*. Make an example of your own as a demonstration. Have each student display his or her design to the class and the class can determine as a group whether or not the design has one or more lines of symmetry.

3. Have students make new designs that only have one line of symmetry and then have them share their designs with the class. Have students make new designs that have exactly two lines of symmetry and share them. Ask students what the greatest number of lines of symmetry possible is. (A circle has an infinite number

of lines of symmetry. Do not tell students this answer right away; instead have them think about it overnight if they do not come up with it immediately.)

4. Have students fold a piece of scrap paper in half, cut out a design, and then unfold the paper. Have students draw the line of symmetry on the fold. Distribute Miras and have students place a Mira on the line of symmetry with the beveled edge down. Looking from the left side, the reflection of the left side of the cutout should be mirrored in the red plastic of the Mira and should match the right side of the cutout.

5. Distribute **Letter Symmetry (Handout 4A)** and display a transparency copy on the overhead projector. Ask students if any of the letters have more than one line of symmetry (H, I, and O have two lines of symmetry, but if O is drawn as a true circle, it would have an infinite number). Have the students draw the lines of symmetry on the letters.

6. Distribute **Lines of Symmetry (Handout 4B)** and have students complete the activity. Encourage the students to look for multiple lines of symmetry. Use the **Lines of Symmetry Answer Key (Teacher Resource 1)** to assess student responses.

7. Discuss whether the diagonal of a rectangle is a line of symmetry. (Usually it is not; teachers can demonstrate this by folding a piece of copy paper on a diagonal. However, a square is a rectangle and in a square, the diagonal is a line of symmetry.)

8. Display a transparency of the handout **Two Kinds of Line Symmetry (Teacher Resource 2)**. Make sure students recognize that the first picture is two separate drawings and the second is a single drawing cut by the line into two parts. Tell students that they both are symmetrical due to the fact that when the paper is folded on the line, the images are congruent.

9. Have students draw a simple design (such as a capital A) on a piece of scrap paper. Have them trace the picture with patty paper, then flip the patty paper over and tape it to the page about an inch away to create a symmetric design. Tell students to draw any lines of symmetry. Have students repeat this process using a Mira. The results should be the same. (If the letter A is used as the drawing, there are two kinds of lines of symmetry—the line between the drawings and a line that runs between the mirror images.)

10. Have students place two geoboards side by side. Make a simple (but not symmetric design) on a geoboard of your own, such as the example in Figure 6.

Figure 6. Example of geoboard design.

11. Have students copy your design and then create a reflection on the other geoboard. Emphasize that the second design is the reflection of the first and that when they are placed side by side they have a line of symmetry.

12. Rotate one of the designs by ¼ turn and keep the other fixed. Place them together side by side. Ask students if there is a line of symmetry. (No.)

13. Have students work in pairs. Have one student create a simple design on a geoboard and the another student create a reflection on his or her geoboard. Check their designs before they dismantle them. Take digital pictures of the results side by side or have students copy them onto the geoboard images on **Geoboards (Handout 4D)**.

14. Distribute **Home Reflections (Handout 4E)** and **Drawing Reflections (Handout 4F)**. Have students draw the reflections of the drawings and check with Miras.

15. Distribute **Mirror Reflections (Handout 4G)**. Have students find and draw each mirror line by estimating. Have students place a Mira between the figures until they see the two figures match and draw the mirror line with a new color. Compare their estimations to the line drawn with the Mira.

16. Introduce **Reflective Writing (Handout 4H)** by printing a word on the board or overhead projector. Challenge students to write it the way it would look in a mirror. Try the words "HOT" and "bad." Ask students why the first word is easier than the second to write the mirror image. (The individual letters in *HOT* have a vertical line of symmetry, while the letters in *bad* do not—when you reverse them, you have to decide where to put the extended strokes of each letter.) Then have students complete the first page of the Reflective Writing handout. Debrief their results on an overhead projector with a transparency copy.

17. Have students complete the second page of the handout. Encourage students to check their work with Miras or by holding the paper up to the light.

18. Ask students to build a three-dimensional structure with 10 one-inch cubes and then build its mirror image.

Notes to Teacher

1. Miras may be new to your students. Give them ample time to explore with them before doing the activities. They are very powerful tools; it is encouraged that you find a classroom set to use with this unit. When using a Mira, place the beveled edge on the paper with the bevel on the side of the given drawing you wish to copy. Students who are left-handed may want to place the Mira on the right side of the figure to be copied.

2. Miras are an aid in understanding lines of symmetry, but students must eventually be able to draw reflections without them.

3. You may continue to practice the mirror writing throughout the unit or the entire school year by printing a word or phrase on the board and asking students to copy it and then write the mirror image. Some students will be adept at this but others will improve with practice.

Assessment

- Lines of Symmetry Answer Key (Teacher Resource 1)
- Geoboards (Handout 4D)
- Home Reflections (Handout 4E)
- Drawing Reflections (Handout 4F)
- Mirror Reflections (Handout 4G)
- Reflective Writing (Handout 4H)

Extensions

The following student activities can be used to extend the lesson.

1. Discuss with students whether or not the human face is symmetric. (Yes, the human face is symmetric in the sense of features, but there are many variations in features that are not symmetric. This is normal.) To show this, find a picture of a person that is taken straight from the front. Set a mirror on the axis of symmetry and observe the "new face." Ask students if the two faces look the same and which looks better.

2. Have students observe examples of symmetry around the classroom or from magazine pictures. Bring in pictures of buildings and discuss symmetry or lack of symmetry in classical vs. contemporary designs. Note the two kinds of symmetry discussed in this lesson.

Letter Symmetry (Handout 4A)

Directions: Draw the line of symmetry for each letter if it exists.

A	B	C	D
E	F	G	H
I	J	K	L
M	N	O	P
Q	R	S	T
U	V	W	X
Y	Z		

Name_____   Date_____

Lines of Symmetry (Handout 4B)

Directions: Write the number of lines of symmetry on the given line for each figure. Draw all lines of symmetry and check with your Mira.

1. _____

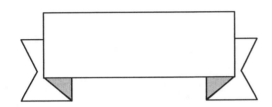

5. _____

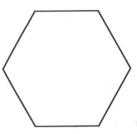

2. _____

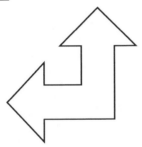

6. _____

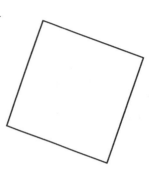

3. _____

7. _____

4. _____

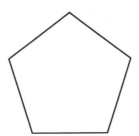

8. _____

Lines of Symmetry Answer Key
(Teacher Resource 1)

Directions: Write the number of lines of symmetry on the given line for each figure. Draw all lines of symmetry and check with your Mira.

1. __1__

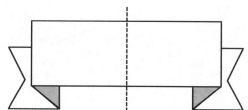

2. __1__

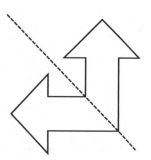

3. __1__

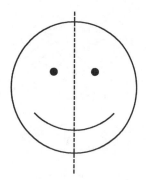

4. __5__

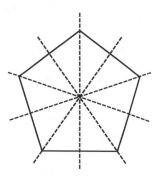

5. __4__

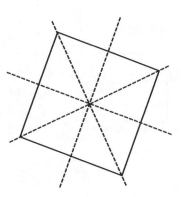

6. __6__

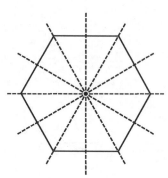

7. __8__

8. __2__

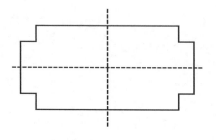

Two Kinds of Line Symmetry
(Teacher Resource 2)

How are the two pictures similar?

How are they different?

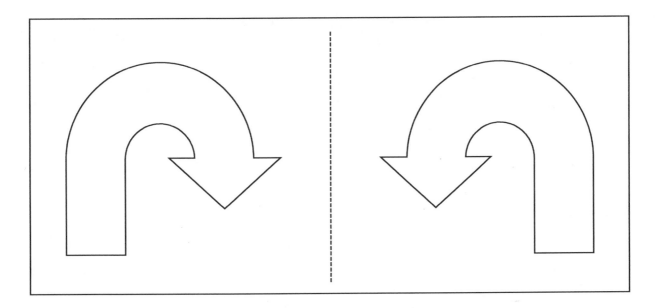

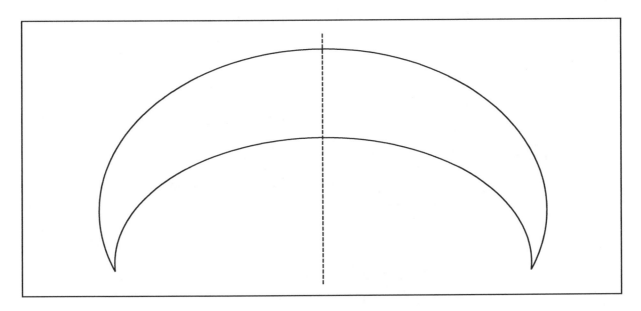

Geoboards (Handout 4D)

Original
figure

Mirror
image

Home Reflections (Handout 4E)

1. Place a Mira on the dotted line. Draw the reflection.

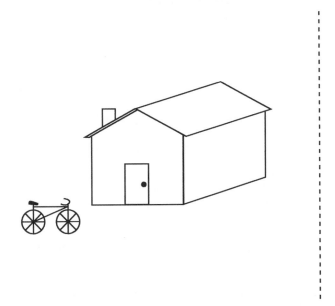

2. Draw this reflection over the dotted line without the help of a Mira.

Drawing Reflections (Handout 4F)

Directions: Draw the reflection of each figure over both of the given mirror lines. Use a Mira or patty paper for one reflection. Draw the other without a Mira or patty paper.

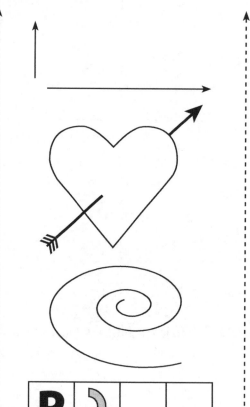

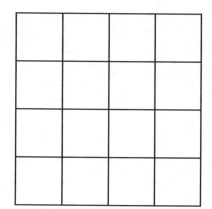

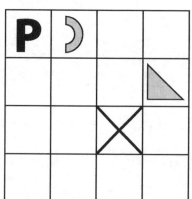

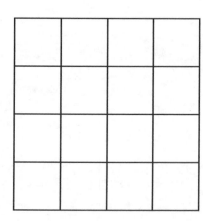

Make a design of your own and draw the reflection over the given lines.

Mirror Reflections (Handout 4G)

Directions: Draw the mirror line for each pair of symmetric figures.

Mirror Reflections Answer Key (Teacher Resource 3)

Directions: Draw the mirror line for each pair of symmetric figures.

Reflective Writing (Handout 4H)

1. Draw the reflection of each group of letters or numbers over the line.

B
C
F
G

2
3
4
5

J K L N P S Z

dog
bread
fright
pack

2. Write this sentence as it would look if you held the paper up to a mirror.

I read about pigs.

3. Write this sentence as it would look if you held the paper up to a mirror.

The red house was cozy and quiet.

4. Print your first and last name. Then write them as they would look if you held the paper up to a mirror.

Lesson 5: Polygons and Tangrams

Instructional Purpose

- To introduce the concept of a polygon
- To measure areas of given polygons using other polygons as the unit of measure
- To create new polygons by the union of two or more polygons by joining at congruent sides
- To explore polygons through the use of tangrams

Materials and Handouts

- Polygon? (Handout 5A)
- Polygon? Table (Handout 5B)
- Using Tangrams (Handout 5C)
- Making Polygons (Handout 5D)
- Polygon Assessment (Handout 5E)
- Polygon Assessment Answer Key (Teacher Resource 2)
- Tangrams (plastic or made from cardstock using Teacher Resource 1)
- Overhead projector set of transparent tangrams, labeled as shown in the diagram at the end of the lesson
- Scissors
- One recloseable sandwich bag per student
- 3 x 5 cards

Vocabulary

Congruent: Having exactly the same size and shape. Congruent polygons have their corresponding angles congruent and corresponding sides congruent.

Isosceles triangle: A triangle with two congruent sides.

Parallelogram: A quadrilateral with both pairs of opposite sides parallel.

Polygon: A simple (no lines intersect except at vertices), closed, plane figure (lies in a plane) bounded by straight sides.

Quadrilateral: A polygon with four sides.

Rhombus: A parallelogram with four congruent sides.

Similar figures: Figures with the same shape (angle measures) but not necessarily the same size.

Trapezoid: A quadrilateral with one pair of parallel sides.

Activities

1. Present the definition of polygon to your class. Distribute **Polygon? (Handout 5A)** and have students cut out the different shapes. Distribute **Polygon? Table (Handout 5B)**. Have students determine which shapes are polygons and organize them on the chart accordingly. Debrief their answers by using an overhead copy of the polygon table and cutouts of the polygons on the Polygon? handout. Tell students to glue the shapes on the table (the polygons include: B, D, E, G, I, J, K, N, and O). Emphasize the essential elements of a polygon including these terms: closed figure, lies in a plane (two-dimensional), made up of three or more line segments, and simple (no segments crossing each other).

2. Distribute one tangram set to each student or use **Tangrams (Teacher Resource 1)**. Tell students that although they may have seen tangrams before, today they will use them in different ways to think about some spatial relationships.

3. Ask students to identify which of the seven tangram pieces are polygons and describe why. (All of the pieces are polygons.) Discuss the names of these polygons. Ask students what other characteristics they notice about the polygons and list their ideas on the board. Have students check for right angles by using a 3 x 5 card. Here is a list of some things that should be noticed:
   - A and E are right triangles that are congruent. They are isosceles because two sides are the same length.
   - D is a right triangle.
   - B is a square, a quadrilateral with four right angles and four congruent sides.
   - F and G are right triangles that are congruent. They are isosceles because two sides are the same length.
   - C is a parallelogram—a quadrilateral with opposite sides parallel.
   - If you line up A or E next to D and then F or G, you have a set of similar triangles. Angle measurements are the same but side lengths are not.

4. Have students put the tangram pieces back together to form the original square. Have a student assemble his or hers on the overhead and describe the steps used to complete the task. Help the student use correct vocabulary when referring to the pieces (e.g., parallelogram or rhombus rather than "diamond"). (Diamond is not a geometric term.)

5. Review the concept of area as the number of square units needed to cover a two-dimensional surface. Tell students that you want to cover the entire square with the piece labeled G. Place triangle G on the overhead and explain that this is the unit for measuring area in the first problem. Ask students how many Gs they would need to cover the square completely. Let students work alone for a short time, then have them discuss their idea with another student, and debrief with the class. Students should explain their thinking.

6. Distribute **Using Tangrams (Handout 5C)** and have students complete the activity in groups with Tangram pieces from **Tangrams (Teacher Resource 2)**. Discuss their answers and thinking as a class.

7. Tell students that their task is to create new polygons from two or more tangram pieces by attaching pieces at congruent sides. For each new polygon they find, tell them to trace the creation on an index card, label the pieces with their letter names, and write the student's name. Encourage them to find as many new polygons as they can using only the seven tangram pieces in the set. Demonstrate these examples on the overhead.

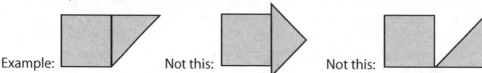

Note: The figure at the left is called a trapezoid because it has one set of parallel sides.

8. Make a polygon table similar to **Making Polygons (Handout 5D)** on a bulletin board and have students attach their new polygons to the table to make a class list.

9. Distribute the **Polygon Assessment (Handout 5E)** and have students complete it. Use the **Polygon Assessment Answer Key (Teacher Resource 2)** to assess student responses.

Math Journal

Have students write a response to these prompts in their math journals:
- Copy tangram pieces A, E, and F in your journal. Write everything you can about these pieces. What names can be used to identify them? What is special about each of them? How are they the same and how are they different?
- Imagine that your friend asks you what a polygon is. Write your response.

Notes to Teacher

1. **Making Polygons (Handout 5D)** is an ongoing project. It is a fluency task. Unlike most classroom assignments, this can give a sense of the long-term nature of how mathematicians keep on working at problems over periods of time.

2. The area activity and the activity in which students create new polygons are good journal activities. Students will then have a long-term documentation of their work on these tasks.

Assessment

- Polygon Assessment (Handout 5E)
- Journal responses.

Extensions

The following student activities can be used to extend the lesson.

1. Let students make their own tangrams by folding paper and cutting. This Web site provides step-by-step directions for creating tangram pieces: http://www.uen.org/Lessonplan/preview.cgi?LPid=11079. In summation:
   a. Make a square out of a piece of copy paper by folding the short edge to the long edge, creasing, and cutting off the extra paper.
   b. Fold the square along the diagonal and crease sharply. Cut along the fold to form two triangles.
   c. Fold one of the triangles in half, bisecting the right angle, to form two smaller triangles. Crease and cut along this fold. Label these two triangles "A" and "E" and set them aside.
   d. Using the remaining triangle, fold the corner of the right angle to the midpoint of the hypotenuse. Crease and cut. Label the triangle "D" and set aside.
   e. Fold the remaining trapezoid in half along its line of symmetry. Cut along this fold, creating two small trapezoids.
   f. Using one of the trapezoids you just made, fold the right angle onto the midpoint of the longest side (opposite it). Fold and cut along this line. Label the resulting small triangle "F" and the remaining parallelogram "C."

g. Using the remaining trapezoid you made in step (e), fold the vertex of the obtuse angle onto the midpoint of the longest side (opposite it). Fold and cut along this line. Label the small triangle "G" and the square "B."

2. Have students use online tangrams at the National Library of Virtual Manipulatives' Web site: http://nlvm.usu.edu/en/nav/frames_asid_112_g_2_t_1.html?open=activities. At this site, tell students to click on the shape that they wish to make and then cover it with the tangram pieces by rotating and dragging them onto the shape.

3. Have students locate three different examples of polygons in your classroom and explain in their Math Journals why each is a polygon.

Name_____ Date_____

Polygon? (Handout 5A)

A	B	C
D	E	F
G	H	I
J	K	L
M	N	O

Name_____ Date_____

Polygon? Table (Handout 5B)

Polygons	Not Polygons

Using Tangrams (Handout 5C)

Directions: Use your tangram pieces to answer these questions.

1. How many of triangle F would it take to make piece B? _____

2. How many of triangle F would it take to make piece C? _____

3. How many of triangle F would it take to make piece D? _____

4. How many of triangle F would it take to make piece E? _____

5.

Use this tangram piece as your unit	How many of these pieces are needed to cover the big square?
A	
B	
C	
D	
E	
F	
G	

Tangrams (Teacher Resource 1)

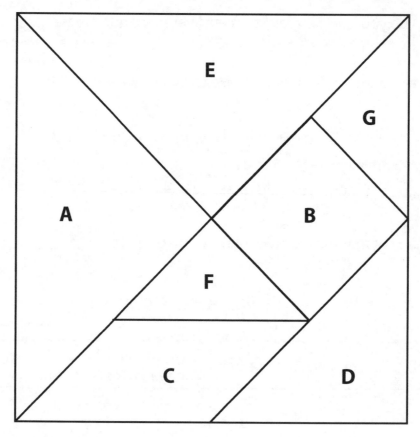

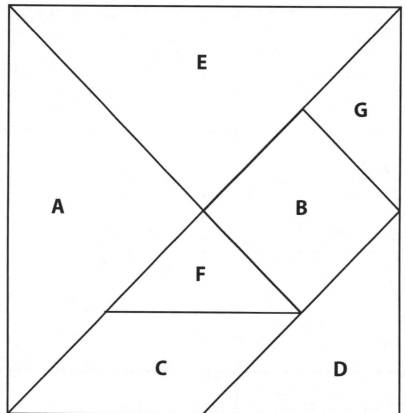

Making Polygons (Handout 5D)

Directions: Use the number of pieces in the first column to form each of the geometric figures that appear in the top of the table. Some have more than one solution while some have no solution. Make a sketch of your solution(s) on other paper (or in your Math Journal). Write the letter names of the pieces in this table.

Use this many pieces	Square	Non-square rectangle	Triangle	Trapezoid	Trapezoid	Parallelogram
2						
3						
4						
5						
6						
7						

Polygon Assessment (Handout 5E)

1. Circle the polygons. Explain why it is a polygon.

 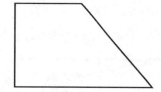 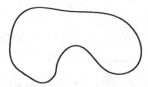

_____

_____

_____

_____

2. Use the triangle below as the unit of area to find the area of the polygon on the right. Show how you know.

Area = _____ triangles.

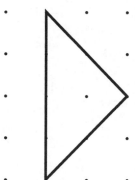 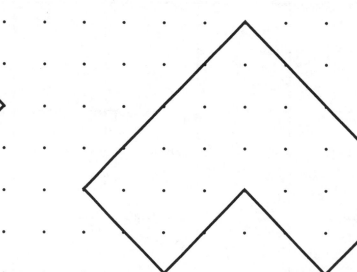

3. Create all of the polygons you can using 1, 2, 3, or 4 of these isosceles right triangles. Connecting sides must be congruent!

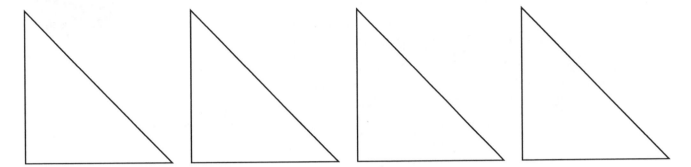

Polygon Assessment Answer Key (Teacher Resource 2)

1. Circle the polygons. Explain why it is a polygon.

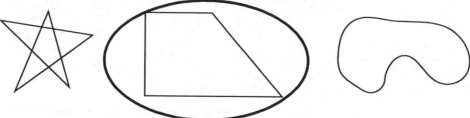

This is closed figure made of more than three line segments that do not cross each other. It lies in a plane (we know this because it is drawn on paper, which represents a plane).

2. Use the triangle below as the unit of area to find the area of the polygon on the right. Show how you know.

Area = **6** triangles.

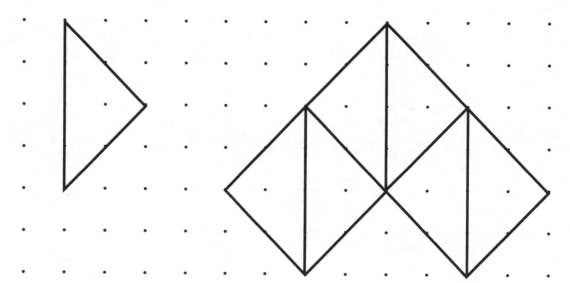

3. Create all of the polygons you can using 1, 2, 3, or 4 of these isosceles right triangles. Connecting sides must be congruent!

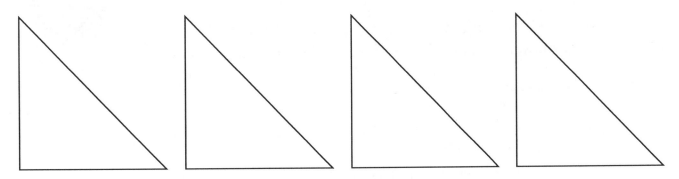

Answers may vary. Here is a complete set:

Using one triangle:

Using two triangles: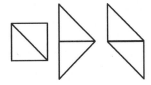

Using three triangles: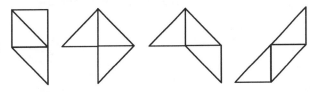

Using four triangles: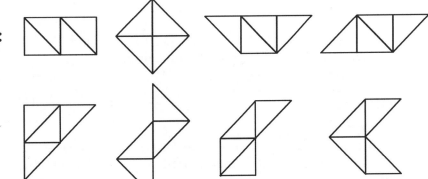

Lesson 6: Polyominoes

Instructional Purpose

- To develop two-dimensional visual discrimination using "ominoes" of various sizes
- To discover the 12 pentominoes
- To reinforce transformations using pentominoes

Materials and Handouts

- 1-Inch Grid Paper (Handout 6A)
- One-Centimeter Grid Paper (Handout 6B)
- Pentominoes (Handout 6C)
- Transforming Pentominoes (Handout 6D)
- Pentomino Transformation Game (Teacher Resource 1)
- 1-inch square tiles or paper squares (about 20 per student)
- Scissors

Vocabulary

Domino: A polygon made from two squares that meet with full edges touching.
Triomino: A polygon made from three squares that meet with full edges touching.
Tetromino: A polygon made from four squares that meet with full edges touching.
Pentomino: A polygon made from five squares that meet with full edges touching.
Polyominoes: A polygon made from any number of squares that meet with full edges touching.

Activities

1. Have students put two squares together with the full edges touching. Tell students that this shape is called a domino. Point out to students that there is only one figure you can make with two squares. Demonstrate on the overhead projector.

2. Rotate the figure 90 degrees. Ask students if the figure is different. Ask students if they flipped the figure over if it would be different. (No.) Make it clear that rotating or reflecting a figure does not make it different for purposes of discovering new dominoes. Tell students that we are looking for distinct ways of arranging the squares.

3. Ask the students to arrange three tiles in as many ways as possible. Tell them that these are called triominoes, noting that *tri-* stands for the number 3, such as in tricycle (that has three wheels). There are only two distinct ways to arrange triominoes (see Figure 7).

Figure 7. Examples of the only two arrangements of triominoes.

4. A tetramino is made of four squares. ("Tetra" is Greek for "four.") Ask students to make as many tetraminoes as possible. Distribute **Grid Paper (Handouts 6A and 6B)** and encourage students to draw their answers. (There are five ways to draw tetraminoes; see Figure 8.)

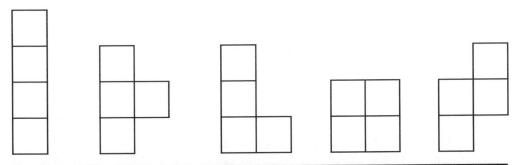

Figure 8. Examples of the only five arrangements of tetraminoes.

5. Have students share their results and explain their problem-solving method. If necessary, mention the trial-and-error process and model a strategy such as the following. Start with a triomino and attach another square to one edge. Record the result on grid paper. Then remove the square and attach it to a new position on the triomino. If this gives a new figure, record it on the grid paper. Continue moving the square to all positions until all of the new figures are discovered and recorded.

6. Have students find all possible pentominoes (made of five squares) and copy them onto grid paper.

7. Distribute **Pentominoes (Handout 6C)** on cardstock or commercial plastic sets of pentominoes to students. Have students cut out each shape.

8. Tell students that the 12 pentominoes are traditionally named after the letter of alphabet that the piece most resembles (see Figure 9 below). Ask students the following questions:
   - Which of the pentomino pieces have a line of symmetry? (I, T, u, v, w, and x)
   - Which of the pentomino pieces have more than one line of symmetry? (I and x) How many does each have? (I has two, x has four)

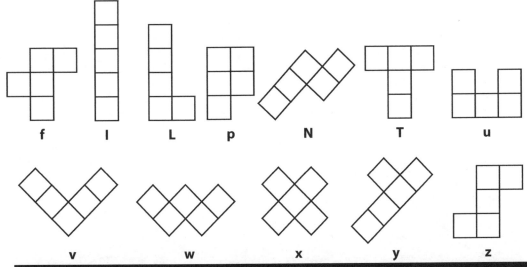

Figure 9. Examples of the 12 pentominoes that form letters of the alphabet.

9. Distribute **Transforming Pentominoes (Handout 6D)** and have students complete it. Discuss their answers as a class.

10. Play the **Pentomino Transformations Game (Teacher Resource 1)**.

Assessment

- Transforming Pentominoes (Handout 6D)
- Participation in Pentomino Transformations Game (Teacher Resource 1)

Extensions

The following student activities can be used to extend the lesson.

1. Have students draw all the hexominoes (made of six squares). (There are 35.)

2. Have students make a chart accounting for area and perimeter of all of the pentomino pieces. (All of the figures have an area of 5 square units and most have perimeter of 12 units except for piece P, which has perimeter of 10 units.) Ask students why this piece has a different perimeter from all the others.

3. Have students cover a 6 x 10 square grid with pentominoes. Have them try an interactive version online at: http://www.math.clemson.edu/~rsimms/java/pentominoes.

4. Read the book *Chasing Vermeer*, by Blue Balliett, out loud to the class. It is a novel-length mystery story that features two sixth graders. One of them carries pentominoes in his pocket throughout the adventure and uses them to decode messages from a friend.

5. To reinforce the letter names of the pentominoes, have students spell out words using their pentomino pieces. Suggestions include pit, flip, zip, put, and nut.

6. If you can find the game of Blokus, have students play it. It uses various colors of polyominoes as playing pieces on a 20 x 20 board. Players take turns placing pieces on the board, each starting from a different corner. Each new piece must touch at least one other piece of the same color, but only at a corner. The goal is to get rid of all your pieces.

Name_____ Date_____

One-Inch Grid Paper (Handout 6A)

Name_____   Date_____

One-Centimeter Grid Paper (Handout 6B)

Pentominoes (Handout 6C)

Transforming Pentominoes (Handout 6D)

A	B	Describe the transformation
Draw the missing picture.		
		Rotate ¼ turn clockwise.
		Rotate ½ turn.
		Reflect over the given line.

Pentomino Transformation Game
(Teacher Resource 1)

1. Put a clean transparency sheet on the overhead projector.

2. Choose a pentomino piece at random from a bag and place it on the overhead projector.

3. Have students choose the same piece from their own pentomino set and trace it on scrap paper in the same orientation as the one on the overhead.

4. Cut apart the squares in the table at the bottom of this page. These are the Transformation Cards. Choose one of these cards and read the directions to students. Ask them to draw the new figure.

5. Draw the answer on the transparency and check student results.

6. Repeat with a new pentomino piece and a new transformation card.

    If you wish to keep score, have students give themselves one point for each correct drawing except for the challenge cards that are marked 2 points.

Transformation Cards

Rotate ¼ turn to the right (clockwise).	Rotate ¼ turn to the left (counter-clockwise).	Rotate ½ turn to the right (clockwise).	Draw a vertical line to the <u>right</u> of the shape. Reflect the shape over the line.	Draw a vertical line to the <u>left</u> of the shape. Reflect the shape over the line.
Draw a horizontal line <u>below</u> the shape. Reflect the shape over the line.	Draw a horizontal line <u>above</u> the shape. Reflect the shape over the line.	Translate the shape to the left. (If grid paper is available, say 3 units to the left.)	Translate the shape to the right. (If grid paper is available, say 3 units to the right.)	Translate the shape upwards. (If grid paper is available, say 3 units upwards.)
Translate the shape 3 units down.	Rotate ½ turn to the left (counter-clockwise).	**Challenge** Rotate ¼ turn to the right and then reflect over a vertical line. **2 points**	**Challenge** Reflect over a vertical line and then rotate ¼ turn to the right. **2 points**	**Challenge** Reflect over a horizontal line and then rotate ¼ turn to the right. **2 points**

Lesson 7: Nets, Drawings, and Mat Plans

Instructional Purpose

- To interpret information about three-dimensional figures displayed in two-dimensional forms such as pictures, maps, and nets

Materials and Handouts

- Drawings (Handout 7A)
- Drawings Answer Key (Teacher Resource 1)
- Mat Plans (Handout 7B)
- Box Folding Example (Handout 7C)
- Box Folding (Handout 7D)
- Box Folding Answer Key (Teacher Resource 2)
- Assessment (Handout 7E)
- Assessment Answer Key (Teacher Resource 3)
- 30 one-inch cubes per student
- Scissors
- Polydrons™ (optional)

Activities

1. Discuss how three-dimensional objects often are represented in two-dimensional forms for convenience. Tell students that a photograph is an example. Have students share other two-dimensional forms representing three-dimensional objects. Other examples include drawings, maps, and architect plans. Explain to students that in this lesson they will work from two-dimensional representations to build three-dimensional objects.

2. Distribute **Drawings (Handout 7A)** and have students examine the drawings. Use the following questions to discuss the drawings. Use the **Drawings Answer Key (Teacher Resource 1)** to assess student responses.
   - How many dimensions does it take to make these pictures? (Two because they are done on paper.)
   - How many dimensions does it take to use cubes to build the structure represented in the first picture? (Three.)
   - How many cubes do you believe it will take to construct the first building? Have students record their estimate on the handout and discuss their strategies.

3. Have students use 1-inch cubes to build the first building. Check and assess students' buildings as they complete them and before they disassemble the buildings.

4. Distribute **Mat Plans (Handout 7B)** and explain that you will call each grid a mat plan, which will serve as a construction guide. Tell students to think of the mat plan as a plan for constructing an office building; the plan illustrates how many rooms to build in each tower of the building. Do the first exercise with students by placing the number of cubes indicated as a tower on the described space.

5. Have students build the structures as indicated in the mat plans on the rest of the handout. Check them as they work and check off the correct constructions. Take digital photographs to use as an answer key.

6. Explain to students that they must think backwards. Ask them how they think they might determine how many cubes are in the cube structures illustrated on the Drawings handout. Have students draw a mat plan for each of the structures in the Drawings handout.

7. Have students make a building of their choice, then make a mat plan for it. Have them hide the building, and then give the mat plan to another student and ask him or her to replicate the building from the plan.

8. Display a transparency of the **Box Folding Example (Handout 7C)**. Have students study the first pentomino on the page. Discuss if the pentomino could be folded into a box if cut out. Probe their reasoning. Cut out the pentomino and verify the results. Tell students that a two-dimensional pattern that folds into a three-dimensional object is called a net. Repeat this same procedure for the second pentomino.

9. Distribute **Box Folding (Handout 7D)** and have students predict if the shape folds into a box. Have students discuss it with a partner and verify with the **Box Folding Answer Key (Teacher Resource 2)**.

10. Have students sort the 12 pentominoes into two groups—those with nets that form an open box and those that will not make an open box. Ask if they see any patterns.

11. Distribute the lesson **Assessment (Handout 7E)** and have students complete it individually. Use the **Assessment Answer Key (Teacher Resource 3)** for grading.

Notes to Teacher

1. Building Perspective Deluxe is an excellent piece of educational software made by Sunburst. In the program, students look at the views of a city block with buildings of different heights in order to predict the views that they cannot see. For more information, go to http://store.sunburst.com.

2. Mat plans are easy but new to students. If they want a more complex mat plan, students are welcome to construct mats with larger dimensions (see Figure 10 below).

2	3	4	1	2
3	4	1	5	5
2	3	3	3	3
1	1	4	1	2
1	4	3	2	1
1	2	2	2	1

Figure 10. Example of a more complex mat plan that can be constructed at various dimensions.

3. Typically mat plans are drawn with the edges of the grid running vertically and horizontally. To get the isometric view of the structure, you may think of rotating the mat plan structure ⅛ turn clockwise.

Assessment

- Mat Plans (Handout 7B)
- Box Folding (Handout 7D)
- Assessment (Handout 7E)

Extensions

The following student activities can be used to extend the lesson.

1. Have students draw on grid paper all nets that form a cube (closed box). This will require making hexominoes. There are 35 different hexominoes and 11 of them are nets that form a cube.

2. Ask students to pick out the nets that actually form a cube online at http://illuminations.nctm.org/tools/tool_detail.aspx?id=84.

Drawings (Handout 7A)

Directions: Predict how many cubes it will take to build each structure, and then build it.

	How many cubes do you think it will take to build this structure? _____
	How do you know?
	Actual number: _____
	How many cubes do you think it will take to build this structure? _____
	How do you know?
	Actual number: _____

How many cubes do you think it will take to build this structure? _____

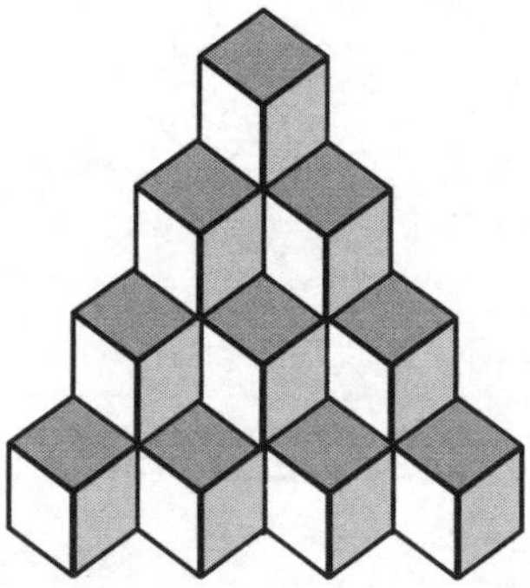

How do you know?

Actual number: _____

How many cubes do you think it will take to build this structure? _____

How do you know?

Actual number: _____

Drawings Answer Key
(Teacher Resource 1)

Directions: Predict how many cubes it will take to build each structure, and then build it.

	How many cubes do you think it will take to build this structure? _____ How do you know? **Answers will vary.** Actual number: __15__
	How many cubes do you think it will take to build this structure? _____ How do you know? **Answers will vary.** Actual number: __20__
	How many cubes do you think it will take to build this structure? _____ How do you know? **Answers will vary.** Actual number: __26__
	How many cubes do you think it will take to build this structure? _____ How do you know? **Answers will vary.** Actual number: __20__

Name_____   Date_____

Mat Plans (Handout 7B)

Directions: Each mat plan gives directions about how high to build each tower of the building. Build each one and have your teacher check it.

<table><tr><td>4</td><td>3</td><td>3</td></tr><tr><td>2</td><td>3</td><td>1</td></tr><tr><td>1</td><td>3</td><td>2</td></tr></table>	Teacher check:
<table><tr><td>3</td><td>2</td><td>5</td><td>1</td></tr><tr><td>5</td><td>3</td><td></td><td></td></tr><tr><td>4</td><td></td><td></td><td></td></tr><tr><td>4</td><td></td><td></td><td></td></tr></table>	Teacher check:
<table><tr><td>4</td><td>2</td><td>2</td><td>2</td></tr><tr><td>3</td><td>1</td><td>2</td><td>3</td></tr><tr><td>1</td><td>2</td><td>2</td><td>1</td></tr><tr><td></td><td></td><td></td><td>1</td></tr></table>	Teacher check:

Box Folding Example (Handout 7C)

If you cut out this pentomino and fold it, will it form an open box? _____

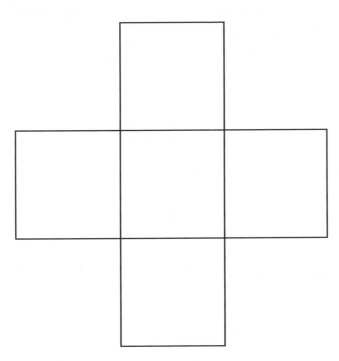

If you cut out this pentomino and fold it, will it form an open box? _____

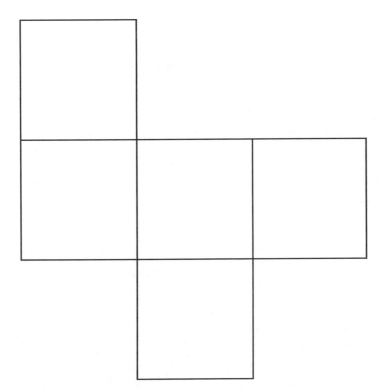

Box Folding (Handout 7D)

Directions: Predict which of the following nets will make an open box when folded. If you think a pattern makes a box, put an X on the square that is the bottom of the box. Check by making them with paper or Polydons™.

1.

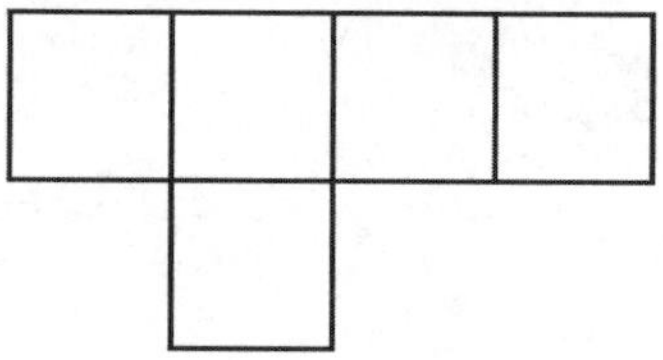

Prediction: _____

Were you correct? _____

2.

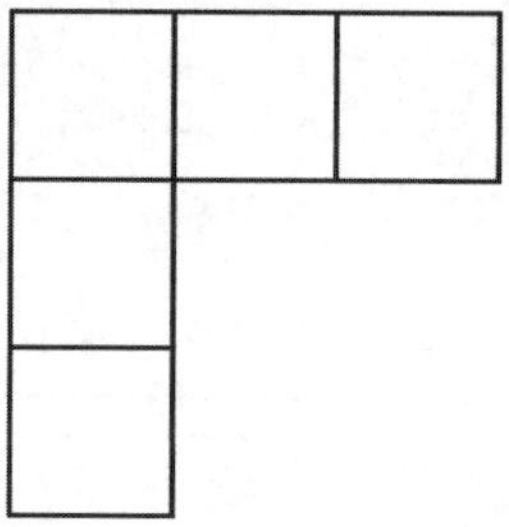

Prediction: _____

Were you correct? _____

3.

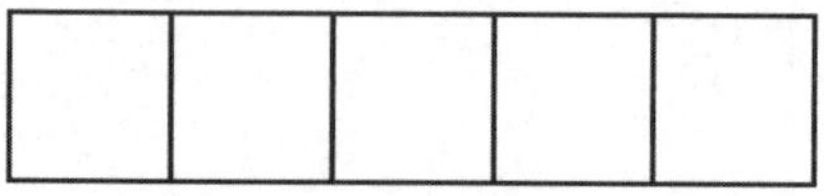

Prediction: _____

Were you correct? _____

4.

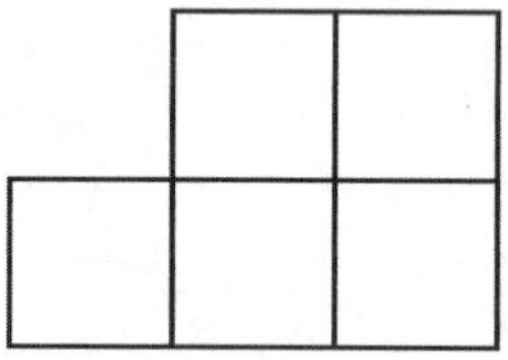

Prediction: _____

Were you correct? _____

5.

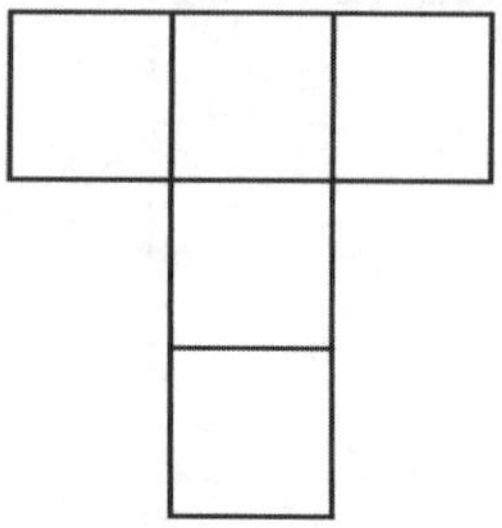

Prediction: _____

Were you correct? _____

6.

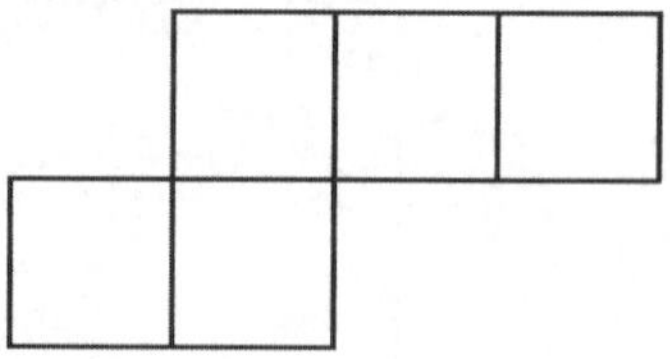

Prediction: _____

Were you correct? _____

7.

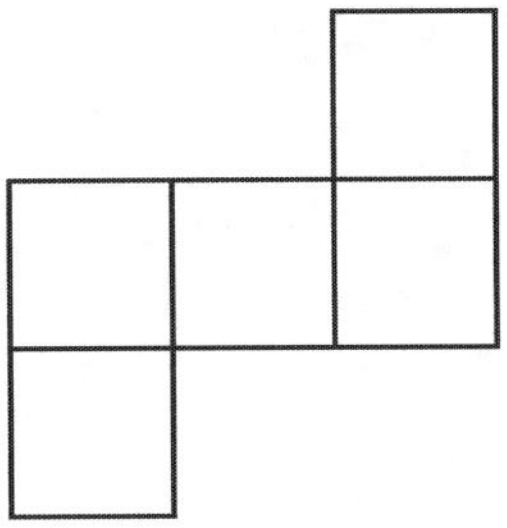

Prediction: _____

Were you correct? _____

8.

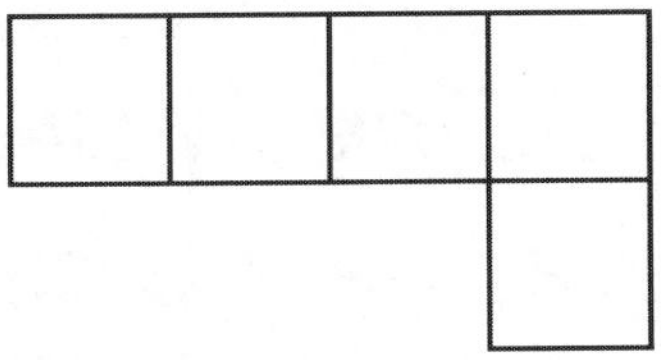

Prediction: _____

Were you correct? _____

9.

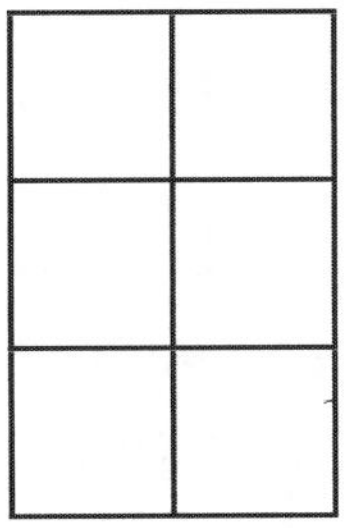

Prediction: _____

Were you correct? _____

10.

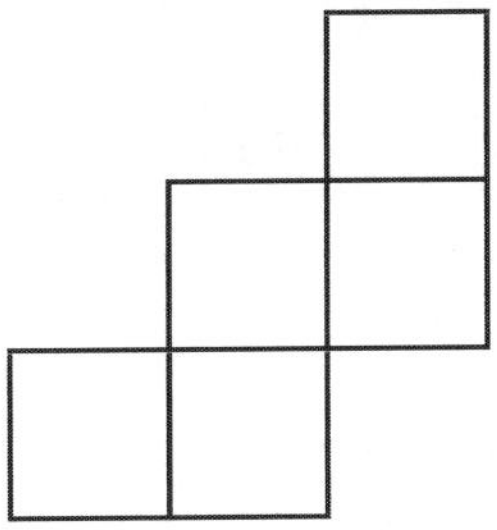

Prediction: _____

Were you correct? _____

Box Folding Answer Key
(Teacher Resource 2)

Directions: Predict which of the following nets will make an open box when folded. If you think a pattern makes a box, put an X on the square that is the bottom of the box. Check by making them with paper or Polydons™.

1.

X

Prediction: _____

Were you correct? _____

2.

Prediction: **Not a box**

Were you correct? _____

3.

Prediction: **Not a box**

Were you correct? _____

4.

Prediction: **Not a box**

Were you correct? _____

5.

X

Prediction: _____

Were you correct? _____

6.

X

Prediction: _____

Were you correct? _____

7.

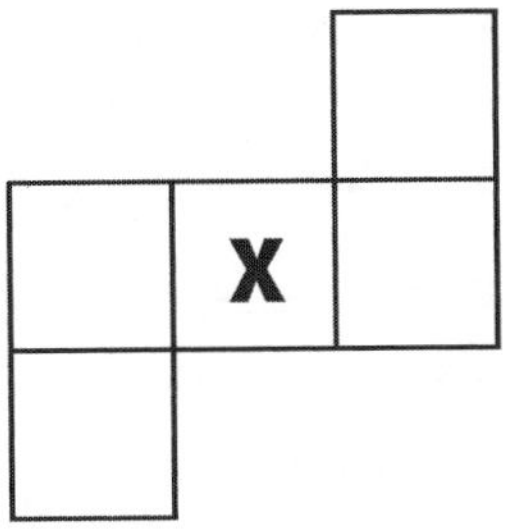

Prediction: _____

Were you correct? _____

8.

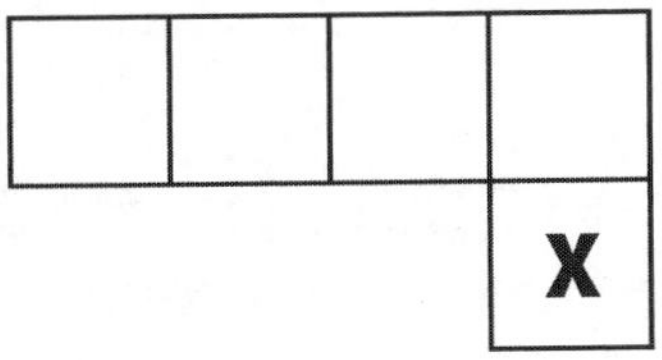

Prediction: _____

Were you correct? _____

9.

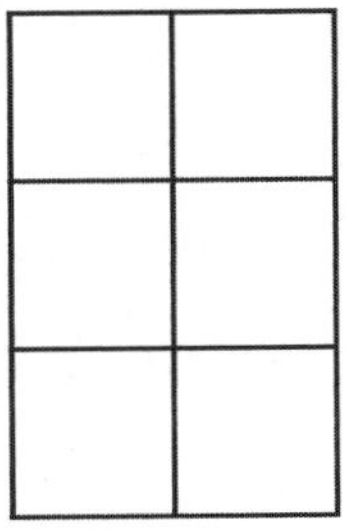

Prediction: **Not a box**

Were you correct? _____

10.

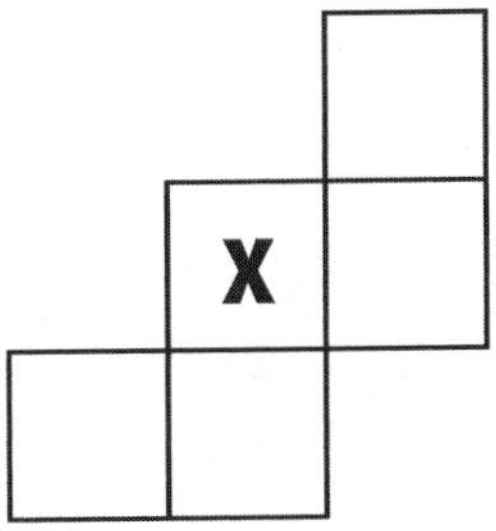

Prediction: _____

Were you correct? _____

Name_____   Date_____

Assessment (Handout 7E)

1. Circle each net that can be folded to make a box without a top.
    Put an X on the square that is the bottom of the box.

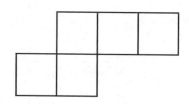   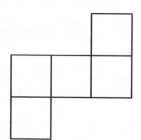   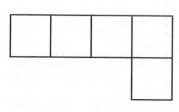

2. Here is the mat plan for a building. Make the building with cubes. Ask your
    teacher to check it.

6	4	1	2
5	3		
4	1		
4			

3. How many cubes are needed to build the building below? _____
    Show how you know.

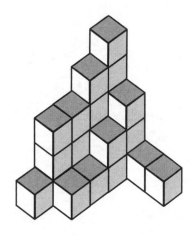

Assessment Answer Key
(Teacher Resource 3)

1. Circle each net that can be folded to make a box without a top. Put an X on the square that is the bottom of the box.

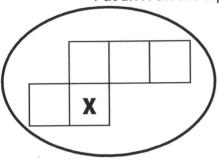

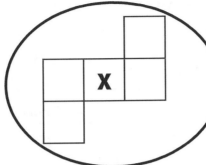

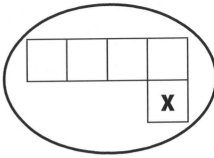

2. Here is the mat plan for a building. Make the building with cubes. Ask your teacher to check it.

6	4	1	2
5	3		
4	1		
4			

3. How many cubes are needed to build this building? __24 cubes__
   Show how you know.

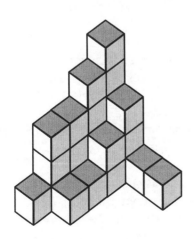

Students will probably do one of the following:

1. Write the number of cubes on the top of each tower and add them.

2. Make a mat plan.

Lesson 8: Projections and Slices

Instructional Purpose

- To observe two-dimensional components of three-dimensional objects by projecting the images onto a flat surface and by slicing objects to observe the cross sections

Materials and Handouts

- Projections and Slices (Handout 8A)
- Projections and Slices Answer Key (Teacher Resource 1)
- Spatial Reasoning (Handout 8B)
- Spatial Reasoning Answer Key (Teacher Resource 2)
- Play dough
- Plastic knives, fishing line, and/or dental floss for slicing
- Fruits and vegetables (knife for teacher to use to slice material)
- Geometric solids
- Items to put on the overhead projector for two-dimensional projections
- Nine 1-inch cubes for each student
- Cubes or other solids made from gelatin (optional)

Vocabulary

Projection: In this unit, a projection is made of a solid (3-dimenisional) object onto a plane (2-dimensional surface). The image or shadow of the object is the projection. You also may project a 2-dimensional object onto a line. Thus, a projection removes one dimension from the original object or image.

Activities

1. Tape newspaper to the front of the overhead projector so that students cannot see what you are setting on the glass. Put a clean transparency sheet on the glass to protect it. Show students a rectangular prism (length, width, and height all different such as a chalk box) by setting it on the center of the projector glass. Tell students that this is the top view. Turn it to its side and tell students that this is the side view. Turn it so it rests on the front and tell students that this is the front view. Ask students to identify the object.

2. Tell students that the shadow or image of the solid on the screen is called a *projection* because you are projecting the image. Remind students that you are looking at a two-dimensional representation of a three-dimensional object. Ask students how many different projections are there for a given object. (Three; there is a projection for each dimension. Use the top view, side view, and front view to identify the three views.)

3. Put a hemisphere from a set of geometric solids sitting on its circular base on the overhead projector. Ask students to identify what possible geometric solids it might be. (Sphere, cylinder, cone, and hemisphere.) Show students the side view and have them predict the front view. Show students the front view.

4. Repeat with a cone and pyramid. If you use a sphere, turn off the overhead projector and put a small piece of double-sided tape on the sphere. Tape it to the transparency so it does not roll. Then turn on the overhead.

5. Project everyday objects on the overhead. Ask students how many views they need to see before they can identify the object. (Sometimes you might know in two projections because the third view is the same as one of the others. For example, a cylinder has the same front view and side view.)

6. Put an object such as a book on the overhead. Show one view and ask students to identify the object. Share a second view, and then a third. Students may not know for sure that it is a book, but they should know it has the shape of a rectangular prism.

7. As with the sphere, turn off the overhead. Put a small piece of double-sided tape on the barrel of a coffee mug, opposite the side with the handle. When you stick it to the transparency, the handle should be aimed upward and therefore not visible in the projection.

8. Turn on the overhead. Tell students that this is the side view and ask what the object might be. Students will not know as the projection should be similar to a rectangle. Turn the mug on its side so that students can see the front view. It should look like a rectangle with the handle attached to the side.

9. In their Math Journals, ask students to draw what they think the top view looks like.

10. Have students self-check their answers while you display the mug upright on the overhead or have students stand over the cup and look directly down onto it. Hint: if you cover one eye you get a flatter image.

11. You can trick students by using a paper cup in this way. Snip a narrow slice out of the side of the cup and then a piece out of the bottom (see Figure 11). Show the front view and side view (both will be the same). Have students draw the top view; when you check they will be surprised as part of the cup is missing!

Figure 11. Example of a cup with a missing section.

12. Tell students that shadows are projections. If you can darken the room enough to make a clear shadow, use a good flashlight and hold it about 4–5 feet away from an object and view the shadow on the wall. Shine the light from the top, side, and front views of the object.

13. Encourage students to bring in objects to project. This will prompt them to look at everyday objects with respect to the nature of their projections.

14. Introduce the idea of slices by bringing in an egg slicer and slicing a hardboiled egg as a demonstration for the class. Before you slice, ask them to draw or describe what the slices will look like. Will they all have the same shape? The same size?

15. Ask students to predict what the slices (cross-sections) will look like when you slice an apple with a knife at various points as indicated in Figure 12. Before you cut the apple, students should draw their predictions in their Math Journals. Debrief regarding the results.

Figure 12. Example of how to slice the apple vertically.

16. Repeat what you previously did but make the slices parallel to the table as shown in Figure 13.

Figure 13. Example of how to slice the apple horizontally.

17. Repeat using a play dough cylinder and cut at various angles (or use Jello made in soup cans). See Figure 14.

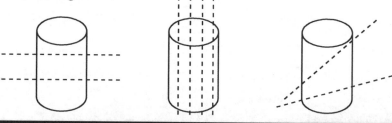

Figure 14. Examples of cylinders cut at various angles.

18. Use the following questions to discuss the idea of a cross-section as a two-dimensional look at part of a three-dimensional object.
    - How many dimensions does the cylinder have? (Three.)
    - How many dimensions does the cross-section have? (Two.)
    - What shape is the cross-section in the first set of slices? (All slices in the first drawing give congruent circles as cross-sections.)

- What patterns do you notice? (All slices in the center drawing give rectangular cross-sections of the same length but the width is narrower as the slices gets closer to the outside of the circle; the slices in the third drawing are not parallel or perpendicular to the table top and they give a cross-section that is an ellipse.)
- If you change the angle of the slice in the third set of slices, what difference does it make on the shape of the cross-section? (The resulting ellipse is stretched out more and more as the angle moves from horizontal toward vertical.)

19. Have students form solids with play dough and experiment with cross-sections made at different angles. They may use dental floss, fish line, or plastic knives to make the slices. Have students report to the group or whole class about their findings and record them in their Math Journal. You may make cubes of gelatin ahead of time and ask students to slice them in all of the ways they can so that the cross-section is a different polygon.

20. Demonstrate for students how a sequence of slices can be used to give information about a solid. Build a square-based pyramid out of clay and cut it into about 5 slices that are parallel to the square base. Then lay out the slices in the order that they were made on a transparency on the overhead projector (see Figure 15).

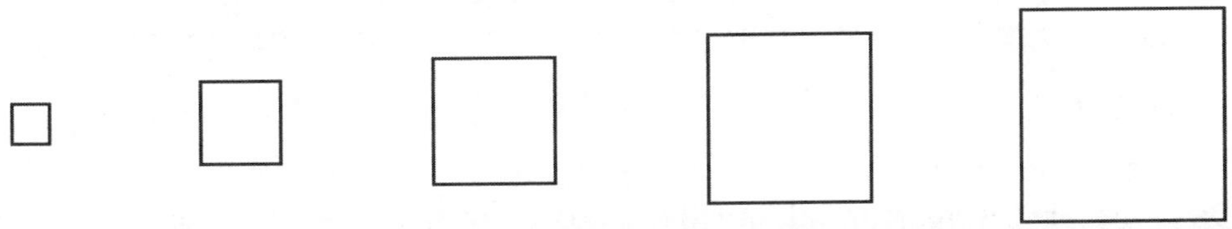

Figure 15. Slices of clay, square-based pyramid.

21. Give each student clay or play dough and a plastic knife (or dental floss) for slicing. Have students form a geometric solid of their choice. Tell students to predict what five slices would look like if they cut the object five times. Have students record their predictions in their math journal. Then have students make five parallel slices and compare them to their predictions.

22. Have students share their slice drawings with another student. Encourage the partner to guess what the original solid looked like.

23. Fill plastic peanut butter jars half full of water for each student or group. Have them tip the jar at various angles and describe the resulting shapes of the water surface. Have students make a report in their math journals about their findings. If you don't have more than one jar, you may do a demonstration for students.

24. Distribute **Projections and Slices (Handout 8A)** and have students complete the handout individually. Use the **Projections and Slices Answer Key (Teacher Resource 1)** for assessment.

25. Distribute **Spatial Reasoning (Handout 8B)** and have students complete the handout individually. Use the **Spatial Reasoning Answer Key (Teacher Resource 2)** for assessment.

Notes to Teacher

1. This lesson may be more challenging to students than some of the earlier lessons. Hands-on experiences are essential. Make sure each student has play dough or clay to try the slicing activities.

2. Encourage parents to have students help them slice foods at home in various ways. Fruits and vegetables will give different looking cross sections depending on the angle of the cut.

3. The following is a teacher-tested and recommended play dough recipe:

Mix together in a pan:
- ¾ cup salt
- 3 cups flour
- 6 teaspoons cream of tartar
- 3 cups water
- 3 tablespoons vegetable oil
- food coloring

Cook over medium heat, stirring constantly until thick. It will pull away from the side of the pan. Store at room temperature in airtight containers.

Assessment

- Projections and Slices (Handout 8A)
- Spatial Reasoning (Handout 8B)

Extensions

The following student activities can be used to extend the lesson.

1. Have students fill clear plastic geometric models with water and tip to observe the different polygons formed on the surfaces of the water.

2. Have students make prints from potato slices and an inkpad or paint. Encourage them to try slices from different parts of the potato (edge vs. center) to see how different the images are when printed.

3. Display a set of geometric solids for students to observe. Play Guess the Solid, using the following instructions (teachers may wish to adapt the activity):
   a. By projecting one solid on the overhead projector and asking students to guess the identity of the object.
   b. By giving verbal clues such as, "I am thinking of a solid that has cross sections that are circles no matter what direction I do the slicing. What is the solid?" (A sphere.)

Projections and Slices (Handout 8A)

1.   Build a cube structure from this mat plan.

3	2
3	1

2.   Use a flashlight or overhead projector to find and draw these projections of the cube structure you made in number 1.

Front view	Top view	Right side view

3. Make a doughnut with play dough and make slices as shown. Draw pictures of the cross-sections.

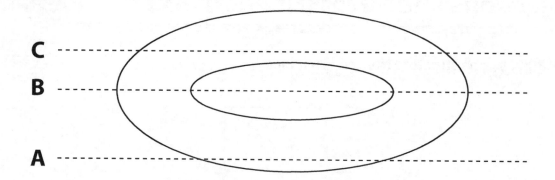

A	B	C

4. With your doughnut sitting on the table, make a slice that is parallel to the tabletop and draw the cross-section below.

Projections and Slices Answer Key
(Teacher Resource 1)

1. Build a cube structure from this mat plan.

3	**2**
3	**1**

Front   Right side

2. Use a flashlight or overhead projector to find and draw these projections of the cube structure you made in number 1.

Front view	Top view	Right side view

3. Make a doughnut with play dough and make slices as shown. Draw pictures of the cross-sections.

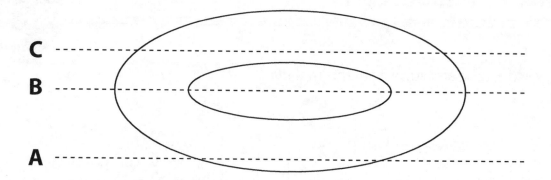

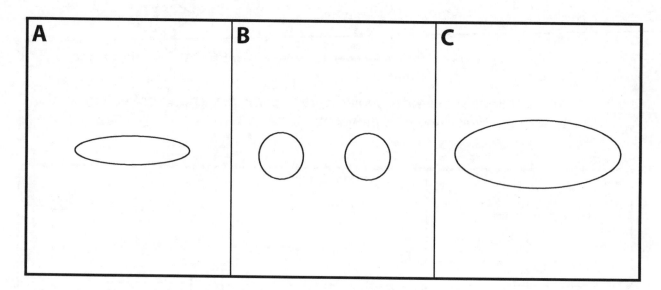

4. With your doughnut sitting on the table, make a slice that is parallel to the tabletop and draw the cross-section below.

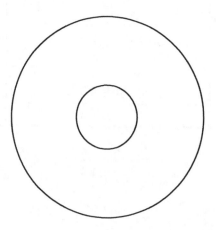

Spatial Reasoning (Handout 8B)

1. Think about the building that can be built from this 2-D picture.

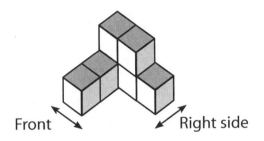

Front   Right side

2. Draw the three views of the building.

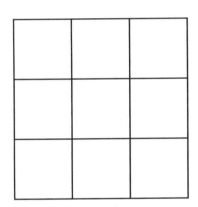

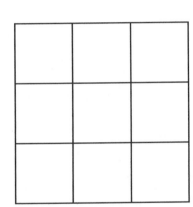

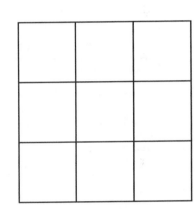

Top view   Front View   Right side view

3.

a. Draw the mat plan for the building.

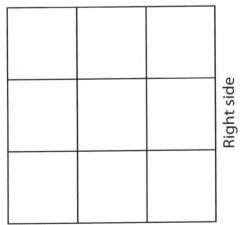

Right side

b. Color all squares of the mat plan that have numbers in them in part 3a.

c. In the space below, copy the polygon made by the colored squares. How many lines of symmetry are there in this polygon? _____ Draw them.

4. A polygon is drawn below. Use reflections or rotations to find all of the different ways to draw this polygon on the grid. Draw all of them on the grid.

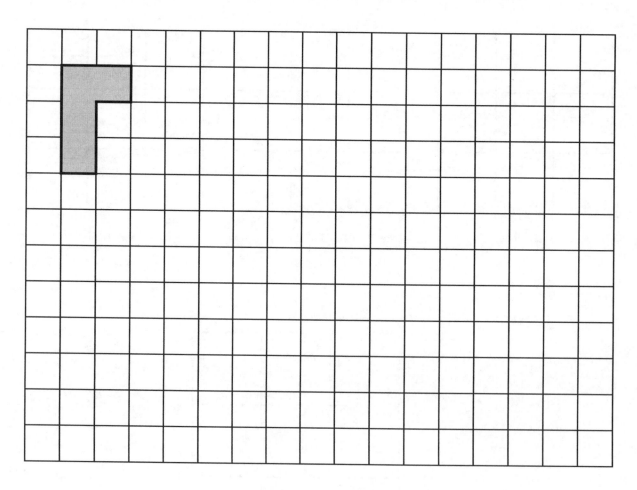

Spatial Reasoning Answer Key
(Teacher Resource 2)

1. Think about the building that can be built from this 2-D picture.

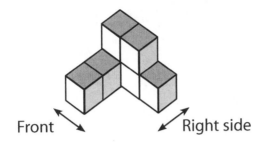

Front   Right side

2. Draw the three views of the building.

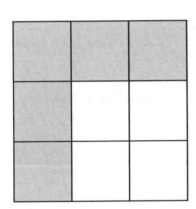

Top view

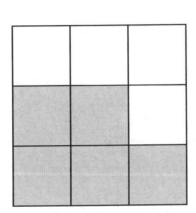

Front View

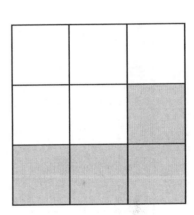

Right side view

3.

a. Draw the mat plan for the building.

2	2	1
1		
1		

b. Color all squares of the mat plan that have numbers in them in part 3a.

c. In the space below, copy the polygon made by the colored squares. How many lines of symmetry are there in this polygon? __1__ Draw them.

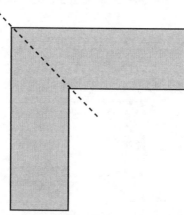

4. A polygon is drawn below. Use reflections or rotations to find all the different ways to draw this polygon on the grid. Draw all of them on the grid.

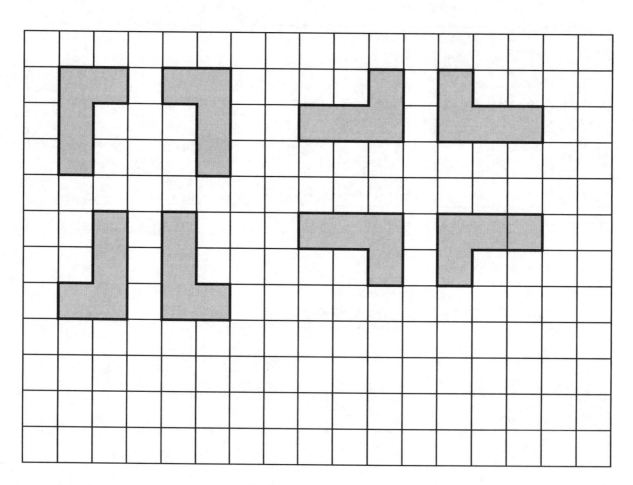

Lesson 9: Postassessment

Instructional Purpose
- To review the major concepts of the unit
- To administer the postassessment for the unit

Materials and Handouts
- Postassessment (Handout 9A)
- Postassessment Answer Key (Teacher Resource 1)

Activities

1. Ask students to list some two-dimensional ways they can represent three-dimensional objects. (Drawing or picture; projection; mat plan; drawings of slices; nets.)

2. Distribute the **Postassessment (Handout 9A)** and have students complete it individually. Collect and score the assessments using the Postassessment Answer Key **(Teacher Resource 1)**.

3. Have students compare their preassessment to their postassessment responses. In discussion, reflect upon what they have learned and how they have grown as mathematicians throughout the course of the unit.

Note to Teacher

The postassessment is parallel in structure to the preassessment for this unit. Change any sets of questions to mirror any changes you made in the preassessment.

Postassessment (Handout 9A)

Directions: Do your best to answer the following questions.

1. One or more of the figures below can be turned to look like Figure A at the right. Circle the figure(s) below that can be turned to look like Figure A.

Figure A

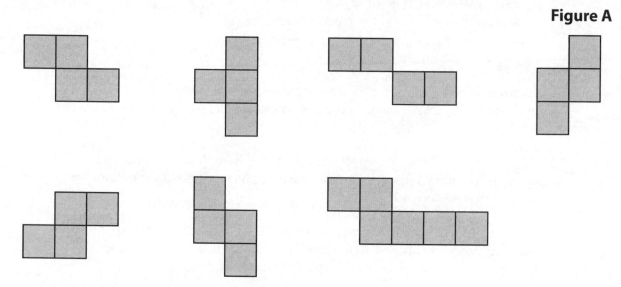

2. Draw all lines of symmetry on this figure.

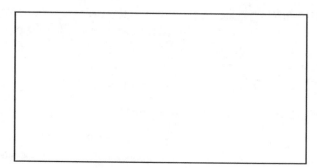

3. Is the figure in Question 2 a polygon? Why or why not?_____

_____

_____

_____

4. Draw the mirror image of this figure over the line.

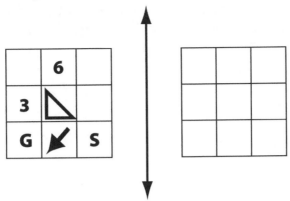

5. How many dimensions does a picture of a house have? _____

6. How many dimensions does a toaster have? _____

7. Look at the pattern below.

    a. If you cut out this pattern and folded on the dotted lines to form a box, would the box have a top? _____

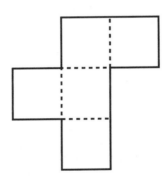

    b. Put an **X** on the square that is the bottom of the box.

8. How many cubes are needed to make the building below? _____

    How do you know? _____

    _____

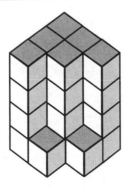

9. Mrs. Nelson put a model of an Egyptian pyramid on the overhead projector and turned the lamp on. Draw two different ways that the shadow on the screen might look depending on how she positions the pyramid.

10. If you cut an empty ice cream cone like this, what does the cross section look like?

Choose the best picture from below:

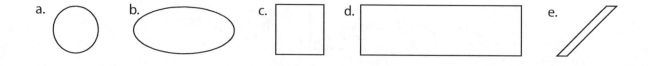

a.   b.   c.   d.   e.

Postassessment Answer Key
(Teacher Resource 1)

Directions: Do your best to answer the following questions.

1. One or more of the figures below can be turned to look like Figure A at the right. Circle the figure(s) below that can be turned to look like Figure A.

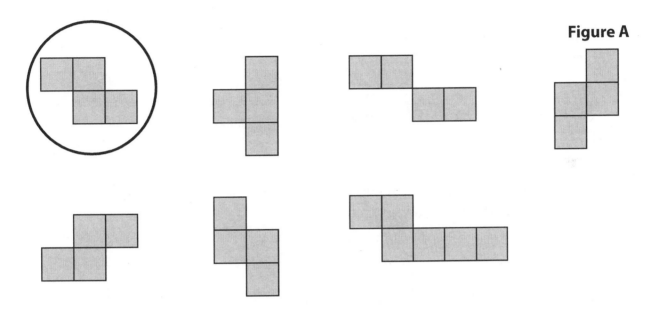

Figure A

2. Draw all lines of symmetry on this figure.

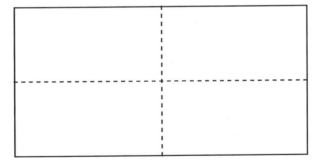

3. Is the figure in number 2 above a polygon? Why or why not?

   Yes, it is a flat (lies in a plane), closed figure made of straight lines. No lines cross except at the endpoints.

4. Draw the mirror image of this figure over the line.

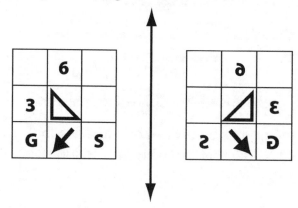

5. How many dimensions does a picture of a house have? **2**

6. How many dimensions does a toaster have? **3**

7. Look at the pattern below.

    a. If you cut out this pattern and folded on the dotted lines to form a box, would the box have a top? **No**

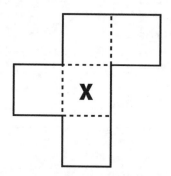

    b. Put an **X** on the square that is the bottom of the box.

8. How many cubes are needed to build the building below? **26**

    How do you know?

    Students may write numbers on the rooftops or describe the number in each horizontal layer. Any reasonable strategy is acceptable.

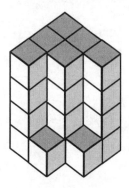

9. Mrs. Nelson put a model of an Egyptian pyramid on the overhead projector and turned the lamp on. Draw two different ways that the shadow on the screen might look depending on how she positions the pyramid.

If it is set down in the usual upright position, it looks like a square.

If it is lying on its side, it looks like a triangle.

10. If you cut an empty ice cream cone like this, what does the cross section look like?

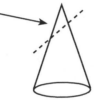

Choose the best picture from below:

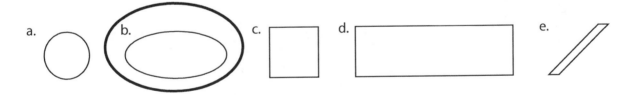

Part III: Unit Extensions and Resources

Unit Extensions

1. Have students complete a jigsaw puzzle upside down so the picture is not showing. Encourage students to describe and categorize the pieces as they look for them. Have students look at more than one puzzle and compare the pieces.

2. Give students pieces of spaghetti cut to the lengths of 3, 4, 5, and 6 inches. Have students make all of the triangles they can and copy them onto paper.

3. Have students view a design that you have created on a geoboard. Give a short amount of time to study it and then hide it and ask students to replicate the design. This can be done to develop spatial memory.

4. Ask students to draw a floor plan of one or more of these:
   a. Their classroom
   b. The wing of the school that contains that classroom
   c. The school
   d. Their house or apartment

5. Take students on a walk in the neighborhood of the school. Then stop and ask them to identify where they are on a map of the area.

6. Cut paper dolls from folded paper so that a string of dolls holding hands results. Show students your model and challenge them to fold and cut paper to match your model.

Unit Resources

Balliett, B. (2006). *Chasing Vermeer*. New York: Scholastic.

Brown, J., & Nash, S. (2006). *Flat Stanley*. New York: HarperCollins.

Carroll, L. (2003). *Alice's adventures in wonderland*. New York: Little Simon.

Dunkels, A. (1990, February). Making and exploring tangrams. *Arithmetic Teacher*, 38–42.

Jamski, W. D. (1989, October). Six hard pieces. *Arithmetic Teacher*, 34–35.

Kriegler, S. (1991, May). The tangram: It's more than an ancient puzzle. *Arithmetic Teacher*, 38–43.

Common Core State Standards Alignment

Lesson	Common Core State Standards in Math
Lesson 1: Preassessment	2.G.A Reason with shapes and their attributes.
	3.MD.C Geometric measurement: understand concepts of area and relate area to multiplication and to addition.
	3.G.A Reason with shapes and their attributes.
	4.G.A Draw and identify lines and angles, and classify shapes by properties of their lines and angles.
	6.G.A Solve real-world and mathematical problems involving area, surface area, and volume.
	7.G.A Draw construct, and describe geometrical figures and describe the relationships between them.
	8.G.A Understand congruence and similarity using physical models, transparencies, or geometry software.
Lesson 2: Introduction to Dimensions	2.G.A Reason with shapes and their attributes.
	3.MD.C Geometric measurement: understand concepts of area and relate area to multiplication and to addition.
	4.G.A Draw and identify lines and angles, and classify shapes by properties of their lines and angles.
Lesson 3: Slides, Flips, Turns, and Glides	4.G.A Draw and identify lines and angles, and classify shapes by properties of their lines and angles.
	8.G.A Understand congruence and similarity using physical models, transparencies, or geometry software.
Lesson 4: Reflections and Symmetry	4.G.A Draw and identify lines and angles, and classify shapes by properties of their lines and angles.
	8.G.A Understand congruence and similarity using physical models, transparencies, or geometry software.
Lesson 5: Polygons and Tangrams	2.G.A Reason with shapes and their attributes.
	3.G.A Reason with shapes and their attributes.
	4.G.A Draw and identify lines and angles, and classify shapes by properties of their lines and angles.
	5.G.B Classify two-dimensional figures into categories based on their properties.
	8.G.A Understand congruence and similarity using physical models, transparencies, or geometry software.
Lesson 6: Polyominoes	3.MD.C Geometric measurement: understand concepts of area and relate area to multiplication and to addition.
	3.MD.D Geometric measurement: recognize perimeter.
	4.OA.C Generate and analyze patterns.
	4.G.A Draw and identify lines and angles, and classify shapes by properties of their lines and angles.
Lesson 7: Nets, Drawings, and Mat Plans	3.MD.C Geometric measurement: understand concepts of area and relate area to multiplication and to addition.
	6.G.A Solve real-world and mathematical problems involving area, surface area, and volume.

Lesson	Common Core State Standards in Math
Lesson 8: Projections and Slices	3.MD.C Geometric measurement: understand concepts of area and relate area to multiplication and to addition.
	6.G.A Solve real-world and mathematical problems involving area, surface area, and volume.
	7.G.A Draw construct, and describe geometrical figures and describe the relationships between them.
	HSG-GMD.B Visualize relationships between two-dimensional and three-dimensional objects.
Lesson 9: Postassessment	2.G.A Reason with shapes and their attributes.
	3.MD.C Geometric measurement: understand concepts of area and relate area to multiplication and to addition.
	3.G.A Reason with shapes and their attributes.
	4.G.A Draw and identify lines and angles, and classify shapes by properties of their lines and angles.
	6.G.A Solve real-world and mathematical problems involving area, surface area, and volume.
	7.G.A Draw construct, and describe geometrical figures and describe the relationships between them.
	8.G.A Understand congruence and similarity using physical models, transparencies, or geometry software.